What people a

Pagan Portals – Demeter

Robin Corak's *Pagan Portals - Demeter* is a book I've been excited to read since I heard it was in the works. Not only does Robin bring Demeter to light, but this author also expands on the often-condensed vision of the Great Mother. By widening the experience of motherhood and mothering, this book creates a strong connection with the reader, a welcoming tone, and open arms. From well-researched content to journal questions, *Pagan Portals - Demeter* is not just for those who have never met this goddess, but it's also for those who seek to deepen their relationship.
Irisanya Moon, author of *Aphrodite, Iris* and *Reclaiming Witchcraft*.

Well-written and thoroughly researched guide to creating a meaningful relationship with Demeter. It is warm, relatable and readable with very good questions posed for reflection and a lot of background information included on the history and celebration of the goddess. If you are looking to delve deeper into working with a mother archetype and psycho-spiritual issues like mother/daughter dynamic, loss and grief, and the mother wound I would highly recommend you include this guide in your collection. I, personally, work with female anger and grief a lot in my psychotherapy practice and found the book relevant and illuminating when linking spirituality, deity work and psychology.
Natalia Clarke, author of *Intuitive Magic Practice* and *Baba Yaga, Slavic Earth Goddess.*

Robin Corak's work is solid and kind, offering readers deep insight into ancient mysteries with a gentle context that any contemporary person (whether a Pagan practitioner or curious reader) can find a place to fit their own experience. Books focused on Demeter are few and far between, and the world is lucky to have Corak's newest text.

Courtney Weber, author of *Hekate: Goddess of Witches*.

Pagan Portals
Demeter

Pagan Portals
Demeter

Robin Corak

MOON
BOOKS
Winchester, UK
Washington, USA

JOHN HUNT PUBLISHING

First published by Moon Books, 2022
Moon Books is an imprint of John Hunt Publishing Ltd., No. 3 East Street, Alresford
Hampshire SO24 9EE, UK
office@jhpbooks.net
www.johnhuntpublishing.com
www.moon-books.net

For distributor details and how to order please visit the 'Ordering' section on our website.

ISBN: 978 1 78904 783 7
978 1 78904 784 4 (ebook)
Library of Congress Control Number: 2021944048

A CIP catalogue record for this book is available from the British Library.

Design: Matthew Greenfield

UK: Printed and bound by CPI Group (UK) Ltd, Croydon, CR0 4YY
Printed in North America by CPI GPS partners

We operate a distinctive and ethical publishing philosophy in
all areas of our business, from our global network of authors to
production and worldwide distribution.

Contents

To my beloved niece, Anam – Such a wise, old soul. You have left quite a legacy of love, nurturing, and acceptance that will continue to impact lives for years to come. What is remembered, lives. I love you.

To my sister, Lisa – You are Demeter in so many ways. Despite having lost a child, you have found the strength to carry on. The advocacy, unconditional love, and nurturing that you have given both of your daughters are truly precious gifts. You are an amazing mother and I am in awe of you. I love you.

To my mother, Sandi – Thank you for never giving up on me even when I didn't understand what it cost you and even when I didn't believe in myself. You helped me to be strong and you taught me what it means to be a good mother. I love you.

To all of you who have been a mother or a caretaker in some capacity, thank you. This world may not always appreciate you but it needs you. May Demeter embrace you and may you provide yourself with the same love, care, attention, and compassion that you have so selflessly given to others.

A portion of the proceeds from this book will be donated to the Angels Like Anam Foundation.

Acknowledgements

As always, there are so many people who have contributed in some way to helping me write this book that I could not possibly name everyone. I will therefore do my best to hit the highlights, but know that if you have crossed my path in any meaningful way at some point in my life, I am grateful for the lessons you have taught me and the ways in which you have inspired me.

My husband Richard and my son Owen have been my champions since day one, urging me to follow my dreams and providing support to make those dreams happen. I am so lucky to have you both in my life. I love you both so much.

I am fortunate to have a family that is filled with unique and amazing people, all of whom have supported me and taught me invaluable lessons throughout my life. This includes my mother, Sandi; my father, Bill; my sister Lisa; my brother-in-law Jimmy; my niece O'Rian, my stepdaughter Emily; my son-in-law Barrett; my grandchildren Zoe and Ben; and my Aunt Linda and cousins Leslie and Tracy. I am very grateful to have you in my life.

To my stepson, Steven Corak, you once again exceeded my (already high) expectations with your recipes for Demeter's Bounty. Thank you for sharing your talent with me.

To Joanne, Marilyn, and Sharon, you welcomed me into your family with open arms 20 years ago and have been so incredibly supportive. I couldn't be more thankful to call you all sisters.

I am thankful for my longtime friends, Jackie, Stephanie, and Benjamin who have cheered me on from the beginning.

To Brian, thank you for your belief in me from the time we were kids until now. You challenge me to challenge myself, and you make me laugh when I am down. Your creativity, free spirit, resilience, and kindness are an inspiration and I feel blessed that you are my friend. Thank you for sharing your kavorka with me.

I am once again immensely thankful for the Sisterhood of

Avalon. My sisters and the wisdom and practices found in the SOA tradition have enriched my life beyond words.

I would like to thank Trevor Greenfield and the Moon Books team for once again believing in my vision and giving me the opportunity to bring this book to life. I am deeply grateful for your support!

To my niece, Anam, to whom this book is dedicated, I love and miss you more than you can possibly imagine. In the far too short time that you were on this planet, you shined so brightly that even the darkest corners of the world around you were illuminated with your love. You taught me so much about love, kindness, and letting go and in doing so you have helped me connect with Demeter in a way that no one else could. You have left an incredible legacy and I feel so blessed to have been part of your life.

Introduction

She is one of the well-known Greek goddesses, but rarely is she presented as a multi-dimensional being. It is true that she is the Mother Goddess and there is much to be learned from her in this aspect. Yet, with over 20 titles and epithets, she is much more multi-faceted than most people realize. In her myth, Demeter exhibits a full range of human emotions-love, compassion, joy, grief, and rage. Demeter straddles the gates of life and death and has much to teach us about not only mothering ourselves and others but also healing our wounds, manifesting our desires, enacting justice, and finding the divine within. In our current world of chaos, Demeter reminds us that nature and the divine provide us with sustenance, offer us freedom from our self-imposed limitations, and present us with invaluable soul lessons.

My first brush with Demeter came through a connection with her daughter, Persephone. As a fragile and extremely shy child with a rare medical condition, Persephone was the first goddess I found myself relating to. Just as Persephone did not seem to be in control of her own life, I, too, had no concept of self-determination and no belief in my ability to direct my own destiny. My family and friends – with the best of intentions – did everything that they could for me in order to overcompensate for my fragile state.

This was particularly true for my mother, and for many years I bristled against her attempts to protect me. Perhaps this was why while I loved Persephone, I was intimidated by Demeter and had no desire to connect with her. In my own life, I had thought that I was angry at my mother for keeping me sheltered when in reality I was angry at myself for relying on everyone around me instead of being brave enough to foster my own independence. This became clear to me when my parents finally realized that enabling me would not prepare me for life and they began to insist that I learn to do things for myself.

It wasn't until years later when I became a mother myself that I began to look at Demeter in a new light. As a mother of my own child with special needs, I began to better understand my own mother's actions and felt a great empathy for her and a deeper appreciation for Demeter. The world can be a frightening, dangerous place. It has been said that having a child is akin to having a piece of your heart go walking around outside your body. I think this feeling is further amplified when your child has challenges unique to a physical, emotional, and/ or learning disability. Like Demeter, we feel an almost primal desire to protect that which we love. However, we know that despite our best efforts, we cannot fully protect our children. There will come a time when they must brave the world on their own and make their own mistakes and decisions for truly how can we ever learn, grow, and fully live if we are not given the opportunity at some point to blaze our own trail?

Myths have always held a special place in my heart. When I find myself in need of healing, understanding, and/or clarity, I often turn to mythology and the deities represented in myths. We can learn a great deal of myths if we are willing to approach each myth as a mystery, a living thing, and are willing to dive deeper than surface level. As Laura Simms states in Kathie Carlson's book, "Life's Daughter/Death's Bride",

"A myth is like an ecosystem. It is more than the sum of its parts...it exists on all levels at once-material, spiritual, ecological, physical... The myth is alive and more close to truth than fact and must be approached like wilderness, on its own terms, to be experienced fully." (Simms, 1997, 19)

Stories are important and they help to shape our own perceptions as well as the world around us. We often find our place in the world through the stories we tell ourselves about ourselves, the stories we tell others, and the stories told to us by others. There is a reason stories have persisted in every culture that exists, long before humans had the capability of writing things down. There are important lessons and great treasures to be found in the stories of old if we are willing to do the necessary work to find this treasure. This is certainly true of the myths told about Demeter.

Demeter can help us to learn how to find the balance between keeping our children close and giving them all of the nurturing, love, and tools needed for the journey of life while also knowing when to let go. Women who have identified solely or primarily with their role of a mother may feel a void or feel lost once their children are grown and out of the house. Working with Demeter can facilitate a powerful journey of self-discovery resulting in a re-envisioning and reclaiming of our potential and our own lives. For those of us who may not have had a positive relationship with our own mothers, Demeter empowers us to access our own nurturing abilities so that we may provide ourselves with the quantity and quality of love that we feel we did not receive. Still, as powerful as she is in her aspect as a mother of children, Demeter's gifts go beyond this one role.

Demeter's lessons can be accessed by all women, regardless of whether or not they are mothers in the biological or adoptive sense. The ability to create and nurture are hallmark aspects of maternal energy and these abilities can be employed in many different ways. I have met many women who were not mothers in the traditional sense but whom were talented caretakers, creators, and leaders. These women – whether consciously or subconsciously – have drawn upon the very energies that we associate with Demeter to breathe life into this world and to ensure its sustainability and growth whether that life happens to be an idea, a project, a piece of art, or compassion and healing for others.

The mother archetype is not just about loving and nurturing, it is also about protection and advocacy to ensure that that which has been given life will survive and thrive. History offers many examples of strong women whose commitment to fostering growth was the spark that lit the flame of impactful movements such as the suffrage movement. These women fiercely advocated for what they believed in and, much like a mother bear protecting her cubs, they ensured that their voices were heard so that the movement could grow and ultimately change the course of history.

Grief, depression, and anger are emotions that Demeter understands very well as evidenced by her reaction to losing her daughter in Homer's "Hymn to Demeter". In many ways, Demeter's journey parallels her daughter's. Whereas Persephone is taken to the literal Underworld before ultimately being reunited with her mother, Demeter must descend to her personal Underworld of grief and depression before she ascends back into the light. Demeter's experiences with her own loss can teach us much about letting go.

Working with the Greek goddess Demeter can help us to find solid footing in an uncertain world. By working with Demeter, we can better understand what it means to reconnect with our own divinity, birth the potential that exists within us, and nurture ourselves and others. Looking back on my own life, I can see that Demeter has in many ways guided my work as an advocate for others through my role as the CEO of a non-profit social services organization and as a spiritual leader within the Pagan community. Demeter has guided me in accessing and cultivating my creativity and the divine within which has contributed to my lifelong dream of becoming a published author. My journey with Demeter has helped me to become a better mother and leader and has awakened me to the power in letting go.

She has helped me to deal with loss and to recognize and honor the necessity of the cycle of death and birth. As I was writing this book, there came a span of two months wherein I lost a beloved animal companion, two friends, and most devastating, my 18-year-old niece, Anam, with whom I was very close. Anam's death as a result of a rare medical condition was entirely unexpected and hard for my entire family to grasp. Grief is a strange, unpredictable thing. In those moments where the waves of grief threatened to pull me under, I reached out to Demeter as though she were a life raft and I found solace and wisdom in Her own experiences of grief and loss as described in Homer's "Hymn to Demeter".

This book integrates research, self-reflection and hands-on techniques to help you connect deeply with Demeter, her story, and her lessons. Chapters 1 and 2 provide an overview of Demeter, her myth, and the various ways in which she was worshipped. This includes a look at the Eleusinian Mysteries and the festival known as Thesmophoria, both of which had a profound impact on ancient Greek culture. Building on these foundational elements, Chapters 3-6 explore the various themes and lessons inherent in Demeter's myth. These include accessing the divine within, healing the mother wound, manifestation and fertility magic, the mother archetype as a powerful advocate for justice, and dealing with grief and loss in a way that can help us to heal and which honors our own divinity.

The remaining chapters of "Demeter" look at how we might work with her and incorporate her wisdom into our own lives. In addition to providing information based on both research and the author's personal experiences, Chapters 3-6 offer the reader hands-on activities such as thought-provoking journal questions, guided meditations, rituals, chants, recipes, and magick related to Demeter. The book provides a full list of correspondences for Demeter as well as information on how to set up an altar and daily spiritual practice to connect with this goddess. All of these activities will help you, the reader, to find in Demeter a strong guide and ally in your efforts to build your confidence, heal past wounds, experience spiritual growth and embrace and manifest the goddess that resides within you.

Now more than ever, Demeter's extensive lessons and her ability to nurture and heal can provide us with the tools to transform our lives, enact societal changes, and achieve greater happiness and self-determination. It is my hope that the information and tools presented in this book will help you to access the wisdom of the Great Mother and experience the joy that comes from walking her path in your own unique way.

Chapter 1

Demeter's Story

One of the original Olympians and the daughter of the goddess Rhea, Demeter was known primarily among ancient Greeks for being the goddess of agriculture and for both initiating and teaching the secretive Eleusinian Mysteries which taught its initiates not to fear the afterlife. Called Ceres by the Romans, the ancient Greeks viewed Demeter as the Mother of all that grew and lived on Earth. She was therefore also linked to abundance and wealth, for assets necessary for building wealth – such as land and the crops that grew on land – were under her auspices. (Reif, 1999). Yet, by contrast she could also be viewed as the goddess of starvation and hunger for while she had the power to provide for those living on Earth, she also had the power to withhold the growth of crops necessary to sustain human life. (www.theoi.com/Olympios/DemeterGoddess.html#Agriculture)

The "Hymn to Demeter" is the most well-known myth featuring Demeter despite the fact that the focal point of the myth in its retelling tends to be placed on the abduction of her daughter, Persephone, by the Greek God Hades. Homer's poems and hymns are often attributed to a menagerie of different and sometimes unknown authors from the 8th century B.C. to the Hellenistic period. (Corak, 2020) Unfortunately, we do not know which author composed "Hymn to Demeter", but we do know that it was likely written sometime in the 7th century BC and that it was likely the earliest written reference to the cult of Demeter at Eleusis. (Shelmerdine, 1995). Perhaps to set the stage for a stark contrast in appearance later in the story, Homer establishes Demeter's great beauty early on in the hymn. Demeter is referred to as being a *"fair haired, holy goddess"* and is called *"Demeter of the Golden Sword"*. (Shelmerdine, 1995). In the translation of the

"Hymn to Demeter" written by author Danny Staples, Demeter is described as having hair that grew in beautiful golden plaits and a face that glows with beauty and she is portrayed wearing a purple robe and a magnificent crown. (Wasson, Hofmann, Ruck, 2008).

Many of the descriptions of Demeter use symbolism connected to the characteristics of the land and/or crops she oversees. The Iliad describes Demeter as having *"assumed the colour of the ripened corn"* when she is seen on the threshing floor separating fruit and chaff. (Burkert, 1985). While some of her descriptions may bring to mind the image of a glowing, beautiful blonde young goddess, many representations of Demeter in classical art and sculptures portray her as a more matronly figure with her ability to bestow abundance represented by symbols such as cornucopias flush with fruit and/or flowers. Some depictions of her show her wearing or holding sheaves of wheat and a torch, the latter of which corresponds to her carrying a torch while searching for her daughter in the Homeric hymn bearing her name.

In the traditional telling of "Hymn to Demeter", Demeter is established as the loving and perhaps overbearing mother of the beautiful yet naive Persephone, also referred to as "Kore". Having fathered Persephone with her brother Zeus, Demeter has kept her daughter protected for all of her life and has made decisions on Persephone's behalf, despite the fact that Persephone is quite clearly on the verge of womanhood. These decisions include but are not limited to turning down offers of marriage from the gods Apollo and Hermes for Persephone. Persephone is said to be out picking flowers one day when she is drawn to a narcissus flower which has been placed there by her own grandmother, Gaia, as a way to assist Hades in his plot to abduct Persephone.

As Persephone moves closer to inspect the narcissus, a hole suddenly opens up in the ground and Hades emerges from the chasm with his chariot. He kidnaps the frightened Persephone and takes her off to the Underworld to be his bride. (Corak, 2020) When Demeter learns of her daughter's disappearance, she becomes distraught and immediately sets off to find her. Line 47 in the "Hymn to Demeter" states,

"For nine days, then, over the earth queenly Deo
roamed about, holding blazing torches in her hands"
(Shelmerdine, 1995, 36)

Demeter is distraught when she finds her daughter missing. She appears to be overwhelmed by her grief and refuses to bathe, eat, or comb her hair. The goddess Hecate arrives with torch in hand to assist Demeter in finding her daughter. Hecate tells Demeter that she knows Persephone was abducted but does not know by whom. They come upon the god Helios who tells Demeter that it was Hades who took her daughter but that she should not worry as Hades will be a good husband for Persephone. (Corak, 2020).

Helios' response only serves to highlight the fact that even though Demeter is a goddess, neither she nor her daughter are afforded the right to make choices about their own lives and/or the lives of their children unless the gods will it. Some scholars believe that the patriarchal dominance happening in ancient Greek society during the time of Homer's writing filtered into religion. As a result, goddesses who were once seen as sovereign became in many cases reduced to consorts or wives of the gods. (Carlson, 1997). According to Kathie Carlson, author of "Life's Daughter/Death's Bride", the abduction of Persephone as believed by some to refer to the *"...male usurpation of the female agricultural mysteries in primitive times"* (1997, 21).

Infuriated with Helios' response, Demeter vows not to visit Olympus and not to let anything grow on Earth until she is reunited with her daughter. She instead goes in disguise as an old mortal woman and while she is sitting in sadness by a well, she is discovered by the daughters of Metaneira, and Keleos, the lord of the city Eleusis. The daughters invite Demeter to their house and offer her a seat but Demeter refuses to sit. Metaneira offers Demeter wine but Demeter asks for a drink of barley water mixed with fresh pennyroyal instead. While no one knows for sure what was imbibed by the initiates of Eleusis, there are many who believe that the drink Demeter requests from Metaneira is the "kykeon", the drink used in the Eleusinian mystery rites. (Shelmerdine, 1995).

Iambe – also referred to as Baubo in alternate versions of the story – offers food to Demeter which she refuses. It is at this point that Demeter is given an unexpected respite – albeit brief – from her grief:

"Until devoted Iambe, intervening with jokes
and many jests, moved the holy lady
to smile and laugh and have a propitious heart,
indeed in later times too she used to please her in her moods"
(Shelmerdine, 1995, 44)

Although Iambe plays a minor role in the hymn, her attempts to amuse Demeter were re-enacted as a standard part of the Eleusinian Mysteries. While this piece of the story isn't as relevant to Demeter's or Persephone's fate, it does play a crucial role in describing how the Temple to Demeter and the Eleusinian Mysteries were established. (Corak, 2020)

Metaneira asks Demeter to nurse her infant son, Demophoon. Demeter agrees to do so. No one suspects that the old woman in front of them is a goddess. Each night when the rest of the family has gone to sleep, Demeter anoints Demophoon with the ambrosia of the gods and places him in the hearth fire to make him immortal. Metaneira happens upon Demeter one evening during this rite, and cries out when she sees her son being placed in the fire. Angry, Demeter snatches Demophoon from the flames and scolds Metaneira, exclaiming humans are foolish and now her son will not be immortal. (Shelmerdine, 1995).

It is interesting to consider Demeter's motives for attempting to grant Demophoon immortality. Perhaps Demeter has grown to care for Demophoon and wishes to protect him by granting him immortality. It is also possible that in the midst of her grief at the loss of her daughter, Demeter wishes to save another mother, Metaneira, from the overwhelming sadness and despair she herself is experiencing as a result of losing her child. Yet her attempts to do so are not aligned with the natural order of things. As author Susan Shelmerdine points out,

"...the tone and focus of the hymn suggest an additional motive: that in her grief, Demeter wants simply to ensure that a mortal mother, who has showed her kindness, Will not suffer the pain she has herself suffered through the loss of a child." (1995, 47)

Shelmerdine goes on to suggest that Demeter's love for mankind and her desire to spare mortals from the pain of loss are at the heart of the Eleusinian mysteries that are eventually given to those within Keleos' realm. Demeter later asks Keleos to build her a temple and teaches the Eleusinian rites in return for the hospitality shown to her by Keleos and his family.

During the time that Demeter resides with Keleos and his family, her depression has caused a famine on Earth which worsens by the day. Zeus eventually recognizes that if Demeter is not appeased, the famine she has caused will wipe out the human race leaving no one to worship the Greek gods and offer them gifts and sacrifices. Zeus initially underestimates the depth of Demeter's anger and sadness and seems to think that sending the goddess Iris to plead for her return to Olympus and an end to the famine will be sufficient. Iris is not successful, so Zeus sends a string of other gods and goddesses to cajole Demeter and offer her gifts and honors in an effort to get her to cede to Zeus' request. None of these efforts are successful. It is not until

Zeus sends Hermes to the Underworld to bring Persephone back that Demeter relents.

This is a very important yet often overlooked aspect of Demeter's myth. As noted previously, the myths of Homer's time tend to have a heavy emphasis on patriarchy and the goddesses are portrayed as not having as much control over their own lives as do the gods. Yet Demeter is able to bring the most powerful of gods, Zeus, to his knees without much apparent effort. As author Richard Geldard points out, to offend a goddess such as Athena could result in the destruction of Athens but to offend Demeter could result in the termination of life on Earth. (2000). Demeter is most revered in her aspect as giver of life but it would be a mistake to ignore that with her power to give life also comes the power to destroy it. Demeter is underestimated by all of the other gods and goddesses, and this causes them potential peril.

Hermes goes to Hades and tells him about the famine caused by Demeter's unwillingness to allow any growth of crops to occur until Persephone is returned to her. Hades is informed that Zeus has ordered Persephone's return as a result. In Homer's version of Persephone's tale, Hades releases Persephone but not before he forcefully slips pomegranate seeds into her mouth, knowing that if she consumes any food while in his realm, she will be forced to return to the Underworld.

Persephone is reunited with her mother, and while Demeter is overjoyed to be with her daughter again, she suspects something is wrong. Demeter asks Persephone if she consumed any food while in the Underworld. Persephone swears to tell the truth and states,

"...But Hades secretly
put in my mouth the seed of a pomegranate, honey-sweet food,
and, though I was unwilling, he made me eat it by force."
(Shelmerdine, 1995, 55)

Because she had consumed food while in the Otherworld, Persephone was fated to remain in the Underworld one-third of the year and would get to spend the other two-thirds of the year with her mother at the onset of spring. Zeus sent Demeter's mother, Rhea, to lead her back to Olympus and Demeter immediately restored the Earth's fertility. (Corak, 2020)

There are many lessons to be mined from the "Hymn to Demeter" and metaphors within the myth abound. Both Demeter's and Persephone's experiences in the myth runs the gamut from joy and innocence to despair and sorrow. Yet, Demeter ultimately also exhibits compassion at various points in the myth. Despite having gone through an arduous experience, Demeter seems to gain wisdom and empathy that can come from great loss as well as perhaps a greater sense of her own power. The "Hymn to Demeter" comes full circle as all that has been lost is regained in some form with the end result being a cycle of birth, death, and rebirth that is played out allegorically through nature each year. Certainly the hymn illustrates the strength of a mother's love for her daughter, the tension and sense of loss that can occur for a mother when a daughter approaches womanhood, and the need for a parent to let go at some point and let their children live their own lives.

Just as importantly, Demeter's story also acts as a metaphor for the cycles of nature. The Underworld was also known as Plouton; a name derived from Pluto, another name for Hades. Plouton was associated with great wealth as it was believed that the Earth's riches were stored below the ground. In fact, crops and seed corn were stored in underground silos during the dry summer months of the Mediterranean climate. (Burkert, 1985). As Walter Burkert asserts, *"Kore is the corn which must descend into the earth so that from seeming death new fruit may germinate..."* (1985, 160) It may be this acknowledgement of a need to let go that provided the rationale for ancient Greek art and alternate tellings of Demeter's myth, both of which portray Hades not as a villain but as a consort of Persephone accepted by Demeter.

While the Homeric "Hymn to Demeter" is the most well-known story featuring this Mother Goddess, there are many other stories that reference Demeter and which provide us a more complex view of her. Demeter is referenced in other literature including Orphic Hymns to Demeter 40 and 41, a myth by Bacchylides, and Hymn to Demeter Six composed by Callimachus. (www.theoi.com/Olympios/Demeter.html) Some of these stories feature Demeter shifting form into other animals. In the Orphic accounts of Persephone's birth, she attempts to flee Zeus' amorous intentions by turning herself into a snake. Zeus follows suit and mates with her in this form. (Athanassakis, Wolkow, 2013). In some of these other stories, we find that Demeter had consorts other than Zeus; some by choice and some by force. Poseidon, Greek God of the Sea, was said to have pursued Demeter in the form of a horse and raped her. The mortal Iasion was known to have "...*lain with Demeter in a thrice ploughed field and was struck down by a thunderbolt of the jealous Zeus*" (www.theoi.com/Olympios/Demeter)

The pairing of Demeter with Iasion is perhaps the most intriguing as Iasion was given a role in the Eleusinian mysteries. Demeter and Iasion's union in a thrice ploughed field is likely a reference to a ritual intended to ensure the fertility of the land. (Caldwell, 1987) Demeter took Karmanor, Lord of Tarrha, as a consort on the Isle of Krete. She also loved a mortal man known by the name of Mekon who had the unfortunate fate of being turned into a poppy flower. (www.theoi.com/Olympios/Demeter)

According to the Orphic hymns, Persephone was the sole offspring of Demeter. (Athanassakis, Wolkow, 2013). However, other stories indicate that Demeter had other children in addition to Persephone. These include her two sons with Iasion; Ploutos and Philomelos, the latter of which was also known as Bootes and was considered to be a demi-god who invented the wagon and the plough. (www.theoi.com/Olympios/Demeter). Ploutos is referred to in many myths as the god of agricultural wealth. As a result of her affair with Karmanor, Demeter gave birth to a son, Euboleos and a daughter named Khrysothemis who was known as a demi-goddess of the harvest festival. (www.theoi. com/Olympios/Demeter) Finally, after Poseidon forced himself on Demeter, she gave birth to two children, Areion and Despoina. Areion was an immortal horse also referred to as Orion. (Reif, 1999) Despoina was revered in the region of Arcadia where there were mystery cults devoted to her. (www.mythologysource. com/daughter-of-poseidon/) Interestingly, Arkadian lore also states that the Erinyes, also knowns as the Furies, were offspring of Poseidon and Demeter. (Athanassakis and Wolkow, 2013)

Other stories both written and in art form show Demeter's capacity for rage and her fierceness in battle. In Callimachus' "Hymn to Demeter 65", Demeter is angered with a man named Erysichthon of Thessaly for cutting down her holy grove of trees and, in the process, killing a dryad nymph who cursed Erysichthon with her dying words. Demeter responded to the nymph's plea by cursing Erysichthon with an unquenchable hunger which caused him to devour himself until nothing was left. (www.greeklegendsandmyths.com/erysichthon.html) An ancient Greek vase painting portrays Demeter with a sword or spear in one hand and a torch in the other as she battles the Gigantes who had waged war on the gods. (www.theoi.com/ Olympios/Demeter)

In one unfortunate story, Demeter unwittingly consumes human flesh. The myth of Tantalus and Pelops tells the story of Tantalus being invited by Zeus to dine with the gods on Olympos. Hoping to impress the gods, Tantalus sacrificed his son, Pelops, cutting him up and feeding him to the gods during the meal. According to Geldard, *"Only Demeter...took a bite before the other gods discovered the sacrilege"*. (2000, 149).

Journal Questions

- What aspects of Homer's "Hymn to Demeter" most resonate with you? What aspects do you find the most challenging to understand or embrace? Why do you think these aspects resonate with you and/or are challenging to understand or embrace?

- In what ways have your life experiences paralleled Demeter's on a metaphorical level?

- If you have children, think about the impact being a parent has had on you. What fears have you experienced as a parent and how has this impacted your parenting style? Did the way you view yourself change after becoming a parent? If so, how?

- Think about a time when you have brought something to life. This could be a piece of art, a work-related project, or fulfillment of a goal you set for yourself. How did this birthing process feel? What strengths or skills did you use to bring this thing to life? How might this experience parallel to birthing and/or parenting a child?

- In what areas of your life do you find it easiest to speak your truth and act from a place of power? In what areas of your life do you find this to be challenging?

- Demeter possesses power that is initially unrecognized by Zeus and the other gods. It is only when her despair triggers her willingness to potentially sacrifice all human life to get her daughter back that Zeus realizes that he must cede to her demands instead of the other way around. What power do you have that you may not have unearthed, enacted, or shown to others? Are there ways in which acknowledging and/or enacting this power might be beneficial? What are the potential implications – good and bad – of enacting your personal power?

- Think about your own cultural heritage. How are women viewed in your culture? What impact do you think these views might have had (positive and/or negative) on how you view your own power?

- The "Hymn to Demeter" is, in one aspect, a metaphor for cycles of nature. What seeds did you wish to plant for the future and how will you nurture them?

- The Greeks planted their wealth in the form of their crops in underground silos during the barren time to protect them from the dry summer heat. The Greeks believed that the Earth's riches were to be found in the Underworld, below the Earth. Think about the times in your life that felt barren and dark or where you felt stuck. Looking back, are there ways in which this time actually protected or helped you to eventually grow? What riches have you found in your own darkness and how can you prepare to utilize future barren times in an intentional and beneficial way?

Chapter 2

Rites, Titles, and Cults of Demeter

Perhaps best known as the Great Mother who provided humanity with the gift of crops and grains, Demeter was also said to have authority over all vegetation with the exception of the bean, which was ruled by the hero Cyamites (www.britannica.com/topic/Demeter) In addition to the titles of Earth Mother, "Dea", "Lady of the Harvest", and "Bringer of Seasons, Giver of Splendid Gifts" attributed to her by Homer, Demeter was also known a number of epithets which emphasized not only her role as nurturer but also her beauty and sovereignty. These included:

Horaphonis – "Bringer of the Seasons"
Polyphorbias – "All Nourishing, Bountiful"
Aglaocarpus – "Giver of Goodly Fruit"
Callistephanus – "Beautiful Crowned"
Eustephanus – "Lovely Crowned"
Eucomus – "Lovely Haired"
Xanthe – "Blonde, Golden Haired"
Callisphyrus – "Beautiful, Trim Ankled"
Dia Thea – "Bright Goddess"
Semne – "Holy, August, Revered"
Hagne – "Pure, Chaste, Holy"
Anassa – "Queen Lady"
Potnia Theaon – "Queen Amongst Goddesses"
Cydra Thea – "Glorious, Noble Goddess"
Agane – "Venerable"
Epaine – "Awesome"
Demeter Panagia – "All Holy Demeter"
Demeter Chioaia – "Verdant Goddess"

Demeter Chloe – "Blooming", "Fertility"
Demeter Antaia – "Demeter Besought by Prayers"
(www.theoi.com/cult/DemeterTitles)
(Mierzwicki, 2018)
(Reif, 1999)

At times, Demeter also was seen as a goddess of health, birth and marriage as well as a matron of laws and civil society. (www.britannica.com/topic/Demeter) She was known as "Amphiktyonis", a title indicating her association with the Amphictyonic League, a powerful council comprised of town-states near Delphi which were charged with protecting the sacred temple there. (www.britannica.com/topic/Demeter) One of the ancient Greek festivals most well-known for honoring Demeter was entitled the Thesmophoria which originates from the terms Thesmoi, "sacred laws", and Phoria, "to carry". The title of Demeter Thesmophoros thus translates to "Demeter of the Carried Sacred Laws" (Reif, 1999)

However, not all of Demeter's titles refer to her reputation as a guardian, protector, and caregiver. Demeter was also known as Cyanopeplus, meaning "Dark Veiled, Cloaked". This title summons a vision of Demeter that seems to align with her appearance as the cloaked, uncomely crone encountered by Metaneira's daughters. In Phigalia, Demeter was called "Melaina" or "The Black One" and was portrayed as having a horse's head; a reference to her shape shifting in order to avoid capture by Poseidon. (Wasson, Hoffman, Ruck, 2008). Such an image of the equine Black Demeter holding a dolphin and a dove was worshipped in a Phigalian cave on Mount Olive along with her daughter, Despoina. (Reif, 1999) Demeter Melaina was seen as the goddess in her mourning state, characterized by grief and loss and bringing barrenness to the Earth. (Reif, 1999)

In areas of Greece such as Arcadia and Thelpusa, the horse-like image of Demeter was seen as a rage filled pursuer of vengeance and was given the epithet Erinyes; a title associated with the Greek Furies. (Burkert, 1985) While Demeter's realm was primarily Earth, she was linked to various constellations including Gemini, Virgo, Bootes, and the constellation known as the Plough. (www.theoi.com/Olympios/Demeter) Many historians including author Charlene Spretnak assert that Demeter was strongly associated with the Egyptian goddess Isis. (1978) In fact, there are many similarities between Demeter and Isis. In the myth of Isis, the goddess comes to Phoenicia disguised as an old woman during her search for Osiris. Taken in by Queen Astarte, she is not recognized, much as Demeter is not recognized by Keleos and his family. Isis agrees to act as a nursemaid for Astarte's son, Dictys. Just like Demeter, Isis seeks to make Astarte's son immortal by placing him in a sacred fire until Astarte happens upon her one night and screams in fear. (Mark, 2016) The Cult of Isis also bears a great deal of similarity to Demeter's Eleusinian Mysteries in that it was very secretive and was believed to have awakened its initiates to the secrets of life and death and eliminated their fear of death (Mark, 2016).

Unfortunately, like most pagan goddesses during the time of Christianity, Demeter was assimilated by the church under the guise of the male Saint Demetrius, Patron of Agriculture. (Carlson, 1997) Angered by this transformation of their goddess into a masculine form, Demeter's worshippers in Eleusis rebelled and created a female saint, St. Demetra. (Carlson, 1997). Unrecognized by the Roman church, St. Demetra was portrayed as a kind old woman with a beautiful young daughter. She was known for feeding the poor even though she appeared to be somewhat indigent herself. (Carlson, 1997)

Cults established in Demeter's honor were widespread. Cults were present throughout Greece in areas including Eleusis, Argolis, Messenia, Arkadia, Attica, Megairs, Aegina, Corinth, Sicyon, Laconia, Elis, Achae, Bolotia, Phocis, Thessaly, Paros,

Thasos, and Rhodes. (www.theoi.com/Cult/DemeterCult. html) Demeter's worship appeared to be strong in rural areas of Greece. (Geldard, 2000) A sanctuary to Demeter was also established on the island of Lesbos. (Reif, 1999) In Hermione, a town at the southern end of Argolis, Greece, secret sacrifices for Demeter were said to take place in a large stone circle. (Burkert, 1985) Demeter's worship was not limited to Greece. Additional Demetrian temples could be found in Scythia, Lydia, Cyprus, Southern Italy, Britain, Rome, North Africa, and Macedonia.

According to Jennifer Reif, author of "Mysteries of Demeter", *"The first evidence of Demetrian Paganism is found in the 15th century BCE in Eleusis, Greece, where its first religious structure took shape."* (1999) Demeter's priestesses were often depicted with snakes, and images of snakes were found on the "cista mystica", the mystery basket that played a prominent role in the Eleusinian Mysteries. (Reif, 1999) Snakes would seem to be an appropriate symbol for Demeter and the Mysteries given their association with transformation and rebirth. There is also evidence that some Demetrian priestesses were called bees, a title given also to the priestesses of the Greek goddess, Aphrodite. (Opsopaus, 2017)

The cults of Demeter differed from other cults in a couple of significant ways. Particularly with her cult in Eleusis, the priests and priestesses were typically chosen from local families. (Preka-Alexandri, 1997) Some of the most prominent positions in the Eleusinian rites were handed down from generation to generation by these chosen families. Whereas cults of Greek goddesses such as Artemis were often served by young maidens, the cult of Demeter was one in which married women played a prominent role. (Breton Connelly, 2007) Married women who served Demeter possessed a level of power not typically found in ancient Greek society and were afforded special privileges. These included special seating at athletic contests. According to author Joan Breton Connelly,

"The most conspicuous person at the Olympic Games was the priestess of Demeter, Chamyne. She had the unique honor of being the only married woman admitted to the contests." (2007, 213)

Men did play roles in the Eleusinian Mysteries but in most Demetrian cults the worshippers were primarily women. While there is some evidence that men participated in some cults of Demeter wearing masks of the goddess, it is also known that there were strict punishments in store for men who attempted to attend women's rites and/or festivals held in honor of Demeter without the permission of the women involved. (Burkert, 1985)

Some of the cults of Demeter also acted as oracles. Prior to the establishment of the Oracle of Delphi, there were oracles dedicated to Demeter. (Opsopaus, 2017) John Opsopaus, author of "The Oracles of Apollo", states that in the second century there existed an oracle of Demeter that would tell a sick person their fate. (2017). According to the ancient Greek writer Pausanias, the sick person would lower a mirror into a sacred spring until it barely touched the surface and would then light incense and pray. After a time, the mirror was pulled back up and an image of the querent – either dead or alive – would be seen in the mirror. (Opsopaus, 2017) Oddly enough, the act of sneezing was considered by some to be an omen or sign from Demeter due to her association with harvest related allergies and the dust that would arise in flour mills. (www. theoi.com/cult/DemeterCult/html)

There were Demetrian cults dedicated to Demeter's chthonic aspects. She was worshipped as a goddess of the Underworld in cults in places such as Sparta and Hermione, the latter of which held a Chthonic festival in her honor. (www.britannica. com/topic/Demeter) This festival included the sacrifice of a cow inside a closed temple and a procession of children wearing garlands of flowers to signify mourning. (Burkert, 1985) Sicilian rulers Gelon and Hieron claimed to have a lineage of hereditary priests dedicated to the Chthonic gods. They established a Temple to Demeter and Persephone in Syracuse in 480 BC as a way of honoring these goddesses in their chthonic aspects and thanking them for looking upon them with favor during the Battle of Himera against Carthaginian forces. (Burkert, 1985)

Just as the "Hymn to Demeter" can be read as an allegorical tale featuring the cycles of nature and seasons, so too does the Demetrian festival season revolve around the cycles of nature as it relates to farming. The festival season can be divided into four time periods: the season of planting, the season of growth, the season of harvest and the season of the fallow period. (Reif, 1999) Each Greek month began on the new moon and lasted for one lunar cycle. (Reif, 1999) Crops common to the Mediterranean climate included grain, barley, grapes, figs, olives, and many other types of fruits and vegetables.

The Greek planting season differs from the cycle that we tend to follow in the Northern Hemisphere. Whereas summer and fall are typically the focal point for harvest in many regions of the Northern Hemisphere, the Demetrian agricultural cycle features a drought in the summer which is considered to be a fallow period. (Reif, 1999) Wheat and barley are planted in Greece from the middle of October to the end of December with blooming occurring in April and the grain maturing in May. (Rief, 1999) Reference to this cycle and Demeter's association with it can be found in various ancient Greek writings including Hesiod's "Works and Days" wherein Hesiod states,

"When the Pleiades...are rising, begin your harvest (in May) and your ploughing when they are going to set (in November) ..."
(www.theoi.com/Olympios/Demeter)

Hesiod goes on to instruct that the wheat that is *"Demeter's holy grain"* be separated from the chaff when the constellation Orion

23

first appears which occurs in July. (www.theoi.com/Olympios/ Demeter)

As the Mother Goddess, Demeter presided over agricultural festivities and her worshippers relied on her favor to ensure that the land would be fertile and crops would flourish so that human life could continue to flourish as well. (Dunn Mascotti, 1990) While there were many festivals sacred to Demeter throughout each year, the two most well-known festivals or rites associated with her were the Thesmophoria and the Eleusinian Mysteries. The rituals celebrated on each of these sacred occasions are believed to be older than the "Hymn to Demeter". (Downing, 1994). This is not surprising given that many cultures had oral traditions that persisted long before they were captured in written form.

The Thesmophoria was a three-day ritual in honor of Demeter which occurred in the fall in ancient Greece. Each day was given a title with the first day referred to as the "Downgoing and Uprising", the second day referred to as the "Fasting" and the final day referred to as "Kalligenia", meaning "fair born". (Spretnak, 1978) The Thesmophoria celebrated the first fruits of the harvest and, as such, the first corn of the season was offered to Demeter. Not only did the Thesmophoria include fertility rites and celebrate abundance, it also honored the sacred laws, or "thesmoi". (Reif, 1999)

The Thesmophoria was observed throughout almost the entire country of Greece and was considered to be solely a women's festival. (Mierzwicki, 2018) Not only was a women's festival unusual, but the Thesmophoria was allegedly the only festival that allowed participating women to leave their homes all day and overnight. (Mierzwicki, 2018) This is astounding when you consider that the women of ancient Greece had few rights and were, for the most part, under the control of men throughout their lives. Outside of the heteira (courtesans), women were expected to remain in the home with married women overseeing all household activities.

There were very few occasions where "respectable" women would leave their homes and when they did, they were expected to be escorted. (Mierzwicki, 2018). With the exception of socializing with female friends, the rare events in which it was appropriate for women to leave their home included weddings, funerals, and religious activities in which women played a role. (https://www.penn.museum/sites/greek_world/women.html) Women celebrated the sanctity of marriage during the festivals and had their daughters participate as well in honor of the reunion of Demeter and Persephone. (Wasson, Hoffmann, Ruck, 2008)

Offerings of pigs were also a characteristic of the Thesmophoria. Pigs and sows are associated with many goddesses, particularly those with chthonic elements. Their association with the cycles of life and death may have been a factor in their prominence at the Thesmophoria. According to Kathie Carlson, suckling pigs were sacrificed by being thrown into pits in the Earth. (1997). This typically occurred on the first day of the festival and in some cases the pigs were accompanied by representations of snakes and phalluses. (Mierzwicki, 2018) Pine branches were also said to be thrown into the chasms dedicated to Demeter. (Mierzwicki, 2018)

Later in the festival, the women would descend into these pits and retrieve the remains of decomposing pigs from previous sacrifices. (Carlson, 1997) These remains would be mixed with seed corn to be used in planting the next cycle of crops. (Carlson, 1997) It is evident that at least in some cases offerings of pigs could be in votive form as a number of terracotta pig votives have been found in shrines for Demeter. (Burkert, 1985)

It has been suggested that the women participating in the Thesmophoria honored a period of sexual abstinence prior to the festival and/or incorporated honoring sexual abstinence into festival activities. Tony Mierzwicki, author of "Hellenismos", states that on the second day of the Thesmophoria, the women fasted and would then lay on beds made up of plants that had a reputation for reducing sexual desire. (2018). On the third and final day of the festival, the women would break their fast with meat and pomegranate seeds. (Mierzwicki, 2018) The Eleusinian Mysteries had some of the same elements of the Thesmophoria but were much more complex and were inclusive of both men and women.

The primary focus of the Eleusinian Mysteries was the separation and then reunion of Demeter and Persephone, the re-enactment of which somehow provided initiates with a greater understanding of death and the afterlife. While this focus was on the individual experience of death, the rites themselves also resonated on a greater cultural and historical level. The book entitled "The Traveler's Key to Ancient Greece" posits that,

"The Eleusinian Mysteries provided a ritual through which the Greeks could re-enact the shift from nomadic to agricultural life, acknowledge their gods in a period of glacial darkness, and be reunited (or forgiven) once again." (Geldard, 2000)

The city of Eleusis for which the Mysteries are named was first inhabited between 1900 and 1600 BC. (Preka-Alexandri, 1997) The Mysteries became a central part of religion in ancient Greece and the temple was actually subsidized by Athens. (Reif, 1999) At one point a famine ravaged Greece, compelling the Delphic oracle to be consulted. As a result of the prophecy provided by the oracle, offerings of first fruits were offered by each Greek city-state to Eleusis as a way to appease Demeter. (Reif, 1999)

The Eleusinian rites were some of the most inclusive in Ancient Greece. Factors such as age, gender, and social class did not impact one's eligibility to participate. Slaves were initiated alongside powerful emperors and philosophers. (Corak, 2020) The only people who were excluded were those who were unable to speak Greek and individuals who had committed murder.

The rites were extremely secretive, to the point where Athens would punish initiates who shared information about the rites with exile or death. We therefore don't know for sure what the Mysteries consisted of but we are able to come up with some general themes based on historical research and archeological evidence. This research and evidence as well as comments from initiates suggest that the Mysteries centered around the worship of Demeter and Persephone and that whatever occurred during the rites strongly negated or eliminated initiates' fears of death and the afterlife that awaited them. Homer alludes to this in his Homeric "Hymn 2 to Demeter" when he says in line 472:

"Happy is he among men upon earth who has seen these mysteries; but he who is uninitiate and who has no part in them, never has lot of like good things once he is dead, down in the darkness and gloom." (www.theoi.com/Olympios/Demeter)

The Eleusinian Mysteries consisted of the Lesser Mysteries and the Greater Mysteries. Initiates were required to participate in the Lesser Mysteries in the spring in order to be admitted into the Greater Mysteries later in the fall. (Reif, 1999) Dedicants in the Lesser Mysteries were called "Demetroi" which translates to "beloved of Demeter" and it is plausible that they were taught to better understand the myth of Demeter and Persephone and how this myth played out in the seasons of nature and life. (Reif, 1999) The ceremonies of the Lesser Mysteries likely had components of purification and consecration. (Reif, 1999)

The Greater Mysteries took place during the first harvests of autumn and lasted nine days in recognition of the nine days Demeter spent wandering in search of her daughter. (Corak, 2020) The "Epoptai" – those who had already participated in the full Mysteries – mentored and supported the first-time initiates known as the "Mystai". Initiation only occurred once someone had first completed the rites of the Lesser Mysteries. (Corak, 2020). While the Mysteries reflect Greek agricultural cycles, the timing of the Mysteries is also a liminal time in that it straddles the light and dark halves of the year and thus lends itself in this way as well to the themes of birth, death, and rebirth. It is believed that prior to the beginning of the Greater Mysteries, the Mystai were required to fast and may even have been prohibited from bathing for a time. (Shelmerdine, 1995). This, too, seems to mirror Demeter's unwillingness to attend to her own self care needs while suffering grief at the loss of her daughter.

A religious figure known as the "Hierokenyx" would announce the start of the Greater Mysteries. (Corak, 2020) Participants would purify themselves and fast as they likely did during the Lesser Mysteries before starting their journey at the Sacred Way. Eleusis came under the control of Athens by the 6th century BC, and this led to the sacred procession from what is now known as the Kerimikos Cemetery in Athens to Eleusis. (Reif, 1999) The sacred way ran from the gates of Athens through the countryside. Sacred objects were carried by priests and/or priestesses of the rites to Eleusis as part of the procession.

Initiates walked from Athens to Eleusis, stopping at various points to offer sacrifices or worship at altars and shrines set up along the way. The walk took some time and it is therefore possible that participants used torches to guide their way as the sun began to set. This would have further connected participants to Demeter as she herself held a torch while searching for Persephone. Once arriving at the Temple of Eleusis, the Mystai's attention would have been directed to the nearby Maiden Well. This well was said to be where Demeter encountered the daughters of Metaneira and Keleos and remnants of the well still exist at Eleusis today. Near the well, a line of priestesses would begin the "Dance of the Kernophonia", also referred to as the "Dance of the Maidens", and this was said to have been the prelude to the rites of the Greater Mysteries. (Reif, 1999; Burkert, 1985)

The Eleusinian Temple used for the great rites was different than many other Greek temples in that it actually allowed worshippers to congregate inside the temple for rites rather than being solely used by priests and priestesses. (Reif, 1999) The temple was decorated with beautiful art showing scenes such as Demeter holding a sheaf of wheat and Persephone holding a crown of myrtle. Statues of priestesses held lustration bowls containing sacred water. (Reif, 1999) The Telesterion which acted as the great hall in which initiates sat was said to have been able to hold over 3000 initiates. (Geldard, 2000) In the center of the inner sanctum was a beautiful painting of the pomegranate trees of Elysium. (Reif, 1999)

Architectural reliefs from Demeter's Temple depict what is perhaps one of the most prominent aspects of the Eleusinian rites – the Kykeon; the sacred drink used in the rites. This drink was given to initiates after their ritual fasting was complete. The drink is believed to have contained barley; an herb from the mint family, and pennyroyal. These are ingredients which make an appearance in the "Hymn to Demeter". The most controversial alleged ingredient is ergot, a psychotropic fungus found in certain strains of wheat. (Reif, 1999) While some historians are skeptical that ergo was a component of the drink due to its potential for toxicity, many believe that the intoxicating effects of ergot were a significant factor in the strong psychological impact the rites seemed to have on initiates.

The Telesterion was lit by dim torchlight and the hierophants of the rites opened the wicker basket known as the "kiste" or "cista mystica" to reveal the sacred objects within. Historians who have studied the Greater Mysteries theorize that initiates were veiled and held an unlit torch and a snake or representation of a snake while a "liknon", or veiled winnowing fan, was waved above their head. (Corak, 2020) The snake would have been an apt symbol for the rites for as we have seen previously snakes are associated with Demeter and are symbolic of death, transformation and rebirth. Towards the end of the rites, Persephone was called upon to emerge from the Underworld cave of Plouton near the Telesterion to be reunited with her mother.

A blade of wheat or ear of corn was believed to have been held up for all initiates to see. The wheat and corn would have acted as symbols of resurrection. Initiates did not simply observe the rites; rather, they also were believed to have experienced the roller coaster of emotions that Demeter felt at the loss of and ultimate reunion with her daughter. According to Kathie Carlson,

"In the Mysteries, human beings too became the seed corn who were mixed with death and sprouted anew" (1997, 25)

Through their experiences during the rites, initiates were able to release their fear of death and be assured of a pleasant afterlife. The Mysteries went on for many years until threatened by the prominence and expansion of Christianity. The rites became forbidden under Theodosius I in 379 A.D. and the temple was finally destroyed by the Visigoths in 395 A.D. (Preka-Alexandri, 1997).

While the Thesmophoria and the Eleusinian Mysteries were certainly the most well-known of Demeter's sacred rituals, there were many other lesser-known festivals celebrated in her honor, all of which revolved around the seasonal cycles associated with agricultural activities. The Rites of Proerosia typically took place in the fall after the Greater Mysteries and were focused on pre-plowing rites, preparing the field for planting, and entreating Demeter for blessings on the crops being planted. These were followed by the Stenia Festival and the Arkichronia, with themes of humor, sexuality and the transformation of Demeter from being barren to being fertile. (Reif, 1999) The Rites of Nestia and the Rites of Kalligenia aligned with Persephone's return from the Underworld and the rejoicing of the reunion between mother and daughter. (Reif, 1999)

The festivals of Haloa and Chloia were somewhat prominent though they did not attain the status of the Thesmophoria or Eleusinian Mysteries. The Haloa was held in what we would typically think of as the month of December. This festival was considered to be a winter fertility festival and incorporated a threshing floor. (www.britannica.com/topic/Demeter) According to Tony Mierzwicki, the Haloa may have also included bloodless offerings such as honey, breads, wine, and fruit. (2018) The Haloa celebrated new beginnings, early successes and gratitude and was marked by humor which sometimes included conversation normally considered to be obscene. (Reif, 1999; Mierzwicki, 2018)

The festival of Chloia was held in early spring in honor of the mothering aspect of Demeter which allowed the grain to begin to sprout. (www.britannica.com/topic/Demeter) Chloia recognized the first rewards or fruits of the season in both a tangible sense and metaphorically as the fruits of one's labor. Success was celebrated and the relationship between mother and child was honored. It is believed that the Greek god Dionysus may have been a part of this festival as well. (Reif, 1999) All of these festivals and rites can help us to better understand our own cycles and the overall cycles of life as well as remind us that even in the darkest of times, resurrection is possible and new life can begin.

Journal Questions

- What rites, traditions, and/or celebrations have you participated in which marked significant periods in your life? Which of these have impacted you in a positive way and how were you impacted? Which of these, if any, do you feel were not helpful and/or may have even been detrimental?

- As we see from Demeter's myth as well as from her rites and festivals, death and life are inextricably entwined and impossible to avoid. This is true in both a physical sense and a metaphorical sense. What little deaths and rebirths have you experienced in your lifetime? Are any of these specifically related to embodying the role of a mother and, if so, how?

- Demeter must eventually let go of her daughter Persephone as she was and reconcile herself to a reunion with a daughter who has grown and evolved. The reunion and rebirth of her relationship with Demeter incites joy and inspires her to once again allow the land to be fertile. What aspects of your life do you feel you may need to let go of? How will you grieve and honor these aspects if/when you let go?

- What things do you wish to birth anew in your life? How will you intentionally fill the void of the things that you have chosen to let go?

- Consider all of your accomplishments big and small. Have you acknowledged and celebrated these accomplishments? If not, why not? If you have celebrated, how can you intentionally incorporate celebration and honoring of your efforts and successes throughout the year much in the way that festivals to Demeter were enacted throughout the year?

Chapter 3

Healing the Mother Wound

It is believed that the archetype of the mother figure comprised the first deity possessing human characteristics that was created or acknowledged by mankind. (Dunn Mascotti, 99) This is not surprising when you consider how much influence and power mothers typically have when it comes to the development of their children. The mother in mythology and in reality, is often the initiator, not just in the sense of bringing forth life but also due to their involvement in the trials and tribulations their children face as they grow older. In her book, "Goddesses", author Manuela Dunn Mascotti emphasizes this point:

> "The mother archetype has perhaps the greatest impact on the collective unconscious of all the archetypes pertaining to the mythology of the Goddess, for it affects both men and women alike and not only in the private sphere, but it touches and influences their social and religious expressions" (1990, 150-151)

When the mother archetype is in balance, children can typically learn from life's challenges in a safe and nurturing environment. Unfortunately, this is not always the case. Often when a mother is out of balance with this archetype, it can cause a ripple effect for subsequent generations of mothers. It is a commonly known principle of psychology that many of the challenges we find repeating themselves in our relationships – including those of mother and child – often relate back to and are rooted in the experiences of our childhood. (Dunn Mascotti, 1990) The ancient Greeks appear to have been savvy to the powerful dynamics of the mother/daughter relationship, for while many myths of ancient times related land fertility to the joining of a Goddess and her lover, the "Hymn to Demeter" and the Eleusinian myths tie the agricultural cycle to the powerful relationship between a mother goddess and her daughter. (Dunn Mascotti, 1990)

There has been much attention paid in recent years to the concept of the "mother wound" and the significant influence that a child's relationship with their parents – particularly their mother – has in the early years of childhood. This is particularly important when you consider that it is between birth and seven years of age when we establish foundational world views that impact later growth. (Dunn Mascotti, 1990) The term "mother wound" has typically been defined by psychologists as the loss or lack of mothering which can include abuse and neglect. Those who experience the mother wound don't receive the love and attention they need as children and have mothers who seem to be distant and less attuned to their emotional needs. (Gaba, 19)

According to Psychology Today, signs of the mother wound may include:

Feeling a lack of approval or acceptance
Feelings of not being loved or not being loved as much as a sibling
Uncertainty about the stability of the mother/child relationship
Difficulties relating emotionally to mothers or mother figures
A need to constantly be better and attain perfection as an attempt to gain the mother's approval and love
A role reversal in which the child feels the need to be the mother in a sense and protect and care for their mother
(Gaba, 2019)

It is not uncommon for women who experience these aspects of the mother wound to have grown up with a mother with mental health and/or chemical dependency issues. In some cases, the woman who cannot relate to the mother archetype unconsciously inflicts these wounds as a result of her own feelings of woundedness formed from her own inability to access the love and acceptance of a parent as she was growing up. As author Alice Miller points out, each of us as mothers can only be empathetic to the extent that we recognize and have healed our own childhood wounds. (Downing, 1994) Regardless of the reason, if not recognized and addressed this wound can greatly reduce feelings of self-worth throughout life and can lead to codependency. (Gaba, 2019). It is therefore critical that, as painful as it may be, those of us who have experienced the mother wound in some way confront our shadow selves so that we may heal from these experiences and ensure that the effects of the mother wound do not interfere with our ability to have positive, healthy, and loving relationships.

Building a relationship with Demeter can help us in these efforts, for she is the most nurturing of archetypes. Demeter can help us learn to mother ourselves, as truly it is only ourselves that we can ever be truly confident will sustainably provide us with the unconditional love and acceptance that we need. Certainly others may provide unconditional love and acceptance at various points in our lives and this is something to strive for, appreciate, and treasure. Yet we cannot control the decisions of others; we can only control our own decisions and thus can only find infinite confidence in receiving love and nurturing if we are committed to loving ourselves.

Working with Demeter can assist us in creating a safe space in which to explore our feelings from our childhood which may be painful. This may include feelings of being ignored, unwanted and/or not valued. By accessing Demeter's unconditional love as a mother, we can learn to validate and love ourselves and see ourselves more clearly rather than through the lens of the mother wound. Just as Demeter fiercely advocated for the return of her daughter, she can teach us to set loving boundaries that honor our own divine selves.

While I agree with the traditional definition of the mother wound, I feel that it is too limiting for there are other types of wounds that can arise from the mother/daughter relationship. One of the most challenging initiations that arises in so many mother/daughter relationships occurs as the daughter starts to mature into womanhood and strives to become her own person. In a similar vein, this happens with fathers and sons as well but may play out a bit differently. Even the best of mothers may struggle with this phase of the mother/daughter relationship for it can be confusing, unsettling, and frightening.

The story of Demeter and Persephone can easily be read as a story about the conflict between attachment and separation. (Downing, 1994) Throughout the "Hymn to Demeter" and in the Eleusinian Mysteries, Demeter and Persephone appear to be defined by each other. They are inextricably tied together. Certainly any mother who loves their child would be outraged at the thought of their daughter being kidnapped and forced to become a wife. This is especially true if the mother does not see her daughter as being of an age to marry. Yet it is important to look deeper within the myth to find the underlying themes that may help us to better understand the depth of Demeter's loss and subsequent grief.

There is a strong bond between Demeter and Persephone. When Persephone's abduction interferes with this bond it creates a sense of loss and an understanding that separation is inevitable at some point. This realization can be quite painful. In addition, the loss of her daughter causes Demeter to question her own identity which has been wrapped up for the most part in her role as a mother. In "The Road to Eleusis", authors Wasson, Hofmann and Ruck point out,

"The Eleusinian goddesses were a sacred duo, often nameless, each related to the other as past and future. Thus Persephone's passage into wifehood seems to necessitate that Demeter relinquish that

identity for herself, for she now disguises herself as a woman beyond the age for child-bearing." (2008, 111)

In this context, one can see how Demeter not only grieves the loss of her daughter, but she also experiences feelings of rage, grief, and depression that may also relate to the loss of her identity. This is something that Demeter grapples with through much of the myth. From that time that Persephone was born, Demeter has made choices on her daughter's behalf based on what she felt was best for daughter. This includes turning down two offers for Persephone's hand in marriage without considering what Persephone might want. In an ironic twist, Demeter is angry with Zeus for facilitating Persephone's kidnapping when in reality Zeus was doing exactly what Demeter has done throughout Persephone's life – making a decision on Persephone's behalf without ever considering her feelings or desires.

It would seem that Demeter cannot accept that she is no longer in a position to make choices for or even protect her daughter. In a subtle way, we can see Demeter's resistance to this change playing out in her interactions with Metaneira's son, Demophoon. When Demeter attempts to make Demophoon immortal, she is not thinking about what Metaneira wants for her son or even what Demophoon may eventually want for himself. Railing against the loss of her own daughter, Demeter tries to make a choice for someone else that really is not hers to make. Instead of mourning for the loss of her daughter and her identity, Demeter attempts to make time stand still and, in a sense, uses her ability to make Demophoon immortal as a substitution for the loss of power she had held over her daughter. (Downing, 1994)

Unlike the Orphic myths, the "Hymn to Demeter" depicts the goddess as not just protective of Persephone but also possessive. (Dunn Mascotti, 1990) Some of this may also be related to loss of her own sense of self and lack of willingness to face her shadow self, for as author Manuela Dunn Mascotti states, Demeter "... *finds in her daughter Persephone the only light for her own inner shadows*" (1990, 169) When we resonate with Demeter in this way, we can find ourselves living our lives through our children, unintentionally eclipsing their own unique spirit and self.

Yet it is also natural for a parent to want to keep their child safe from harm and pain.

Fear of loss can be a powerful thing. Elizabeth Stone once said that having a child is like having your heart go walking around outside of your body. As parents, we do this, knowing that despite our best efforts, we cannot always be there to protect our children. As painful as it may be for us to see, our children must experience the heartaches and challenges that life brings us in our quest for learning, growth, and ultimately transition into adulthood. The protective and perhaps sometimes overbearing nature of Demeter is therefore relatable and understandable for many women.

A lack of balance in the mother archetype and/or an over-identification with Demeter's possessive aspects can manifest in many ways. Jean Shinoda Bolen, author of "Goddesses in Everywoman: A New Psychology of Women" believes that all women tend to gravitate or resonate strongly with one or more mythological archetypes. If this archetype is in balance within us, we can enact the highest, most positive qualities of the goddess(es) we resonate with. However, if the archetype is not in balance due to lack of connection or, more frequently, over-identification, the consequences can be damaging to our relationships and our own sense of self and well-being.

Women who relate strongly with the Demeter archetype tend to have a deep need to become mothers or nurturers in some capacity. This could manifest through pregnancy, but could also involve providing physical or emotional nourishment to others or bringing a project or a piece of art to life. (Shinoda Bolen, 1990)

38

Demeter archetypes may find themselves drawn to vocation such as counseling, health care, teaching, or social work. (Shinoda Bolen, 1990) Other traits of the Demeter archetype may include:

Empathy/Deep Feelers
Extraversion
Depression
Nurturing
Generosity
Supportive
Helpful
Grounded
Dependable
Loyal
Stubborn
Fosters Dependency
(Shinoda Bolen, 1990)

As with any archetype, these characteristics can run a wide spectrum depending on whether or not the archetype is in balance. When in balance, the Demeter archetype can provide an environment for whomever or whatever she is mothering to flourish. When out of balance, the Demeter mother can be critical, demanding, withholding, and driven by fear of loss. (Shinoda Bolen, 1990) She may have difficulty saying "no" to others and may find it difficult to establish healthy boundaries to the point where she becomes co-dependent and/or loses herself and her identity in the effort to care for those around her. She may also see herself as a martyr.

A Demeter mother often needs to feel that she is needed. As a result, she may consciously or unconsciously expect her children to remain in a dependent role, reliant on her even after they have grown out of childhood. (Shinoda Bolen, 1990) It is sometimes hard for a Demeter mother archetype to clearly see how her overbearing actions might be negatively impacting her child(ren) because in her mind she is simply trying to do what she feels is best for her children and keep them protected. Therefore, if her children end up resenting her or pushing her away, it can cause her a great deal of pain and confusion. (Shinda Bolen, 1999)

Unfortunately our society tends to facilitate this type of co-dependency by expecting mothers to consistently put others first, even if it results in sacrificing themselves in some way. Sharon Blackie, author of "If Women Rose Rooted" points out,

"The Earth Mother is the archetype that women are supposed to be in our culture – someone who is self-effacing, deeply nourishing, who puts herself aside in order to give all of herself to nurturing others. This is the archetype which our culture deifies, which tells us what a mother should be." (2019, 206)

It is therefore not surprising that so many mothers seem to struggle with prioritizing their own well-being and pursuing the things that bring them fulfillment and happiness. These efforts are necessary for if we as mothers are not healthy and happy how can we possibly give the best of ourselves to those who rely on us for nourishment? Still, it is not uncommon for women who are mothers or who act as caretakers and nurturers in some other way to feel guilty, as though taking care of one's self is a purely selfish act.

Sometimes the very natural instinct to protect becomes an instinct to possess, albeit often unconsciously. Bolen points out that some Demeter women fear that something bad will happen to their child and thus go out of their way to anticipate and stave off any possible harm. In doing so, the Demeter aligned mother will enable the child and unintentionally limit the child's independence. (Shinoda Bolen, 1990).

I have found this to be true in my own experiences as both a vulnerable, fragile child with a chronic medical condition and as the mother of a special needs child. Fortunately my parents realized early on that allowing me to be overly dependent on family and friends for even the simplest things that I was certainly capable of doing would be detrimental in the long run. Although I rebelled at first at having to do things for myself and for not being coddled, ultimately, I fought hard for my independence and have been stronger for it. My childhood experiences greatly helped me to navigate the challenges of parenting a child who was also vulnerable, albeit in different ways. Without my childhood experiences, it would have been very tempting for me to want to overprotect my child and try to make things easier for him even when this may not have been in his best interests in the long run. Because of my experiences as a child, I was better able to understand and appreciate the necessity to find a balance between caring for and protecting my child while also providing him with space to grow and make mistakes in order to foster his independence.

Regardless of whether or not we have unique circumstances or special needs, just as every mother at some point must prepare for the empty nest, every daughter goes through the experience of cutting the cord in some way shape or form and moving outside of her mother's shadow into her own light. As an adolescent testing our boundaries and straddling the gap between childhood and womanhood, we often don't understand or see the ways in which the separation process impacts our mothers. How can we when we ourselves are grappling with similar feelings of loss, confusion, fear, and uncertainty? The natural desire to figure out who we are outside of the context of being a child reliant on our parents and the urge to claim our own sovereignty propels us through this initiation period. It often isn't until years later that we understand that while this process is necessary and exhilarating at times, it is also a painful process of loss and letting go for all parties involved.

Demeter's myth acknowledges these feelings of loss and grief.

Despite being a goddess, Demeter experiences emotions that are very human and at various points in her story she exhibits characteristics of a human suffering from depression and pain. Taken as a whole, however, Demeter's story also teaches us about the need for independence, self-sufficiency, and finding our own way. (Carlson, 1997). This is true for both mother and daughter as both must redefine who they are in the absence of the other.

In "Demeter's Folly", Polly Young Eisendrath states that Demeter's story seems to say,

> *"Find a way through your own personal awareness and identity to discover a deeper meaning in human loss than a simple ending. Build a temple, practice a ritual, embrace many possibilities and you will apprehend a new perspective on human life and death." (Downing, 1994, 217)*

As daughters, we must intentionally envision who we are, who we want to be and what we want now that our lives have changed. We must build a strong, sincere center that will carry us through any challenges or experiences that make us question who we are. (Downing, 1994) We must commit to living from a place of authenticity, for that is a critical piece of claiming and maintaining our personal power.

From the perspective of the Demeter aligned mother, there are two major life transitions that have a deep impact: the transition from maiden and mother to crone and the time of life when her children move out of the house and establish their own independence. Menopause can leave the Demeter archetype feeling lost and uncertain of her role, particularly when it occurs at the same time that she is experiencing empty nest syndrome. These changes usually lead to one of two paths – either an extended period of depression and feeling lost or stuck, or, positive change, a redefining of one's self, and an embracing of one's personal power. (Shinoda Bolen, 1990)

If the Demeter aligned mother is unable to deal with the loss associated with the empty nest and/or menopause, she may become "...*a personification of the grieving goddess who searched fruitlessly over the earth for Persephone*". (Shinoda Bolen, 1990, 193) If she is able to make her way through this darkness, the Demeter aligned mother may acquire a wisdom that not only makes her a better mother but also provides her with more life satisfaction and enjoyment. She may also learn that there are many ways to "mother". In the depths of her depression, Demeter gave birth to one of the greatest treasures of Ancient Greek religion – the Eleusinian Mysteries. Demeter mothers who are able to work through their feelings of loss can become some of the most effective leaders. When using their wisdom and honoring boundaries, these women are able to help to bring out the best in others and facilitate their personal and/or professional growth.

Demeter can be a very healing, wise ally as we navigate these transitions. Just as Demeter was able to embrace her personal power and stand up to the most powerful of Greek gods, we too must learn to establish healthy boundaries, stand our ground and learn to say no when something does not serve us. Demeter can help us to learn how to express our anger in a healthy way, to attend to our own needs, and to cultivate self-love and self-caretaking. (Shinoda Bolen, 1990) We can learn to bring new life in what may seem to be barren fields through our creativity and talents.

Just as we nourish others, Demeter can guide us in turning our maternal instinct inwards. We must love and mother ourselves with the same intensity and commitment as we have given to our children and/or others that we have cared for. Demeter's myth can help us learn how to birth our own potential, how to advocate fiercely for ourselves, and how to be our own safe harbor by providing ourselves with unconditional love.

Finally, we can allow ourselves permission to acknowledge and grieve that which is lost. We can learn how to deal with loss, not by substituting something new to fill the void of what was lost but by first facing and feeling our loss. Just as a gardener must clear away plants that have died and prepare the soil for a new cycle, we must grieve that which is lost before we can plant new seeds. This allows us time to really think about what we want for the next phase of our lives and what lessons we have learned that will serve us as we move forward.

Too often, we don't speak of the separation that occurs when our children move on and become adults in their own right. As author Christine Downing states,

"Perhaps the greatest tragedy in our culture is that we don't consciously deal with separation. We do not have rituals to support our movement away from mothers. We do not have rituals to support mothers in letting go of their daughters. Nor do we have rituals for either mothers or daughters that support their definition of self as women in the world." (1994, 183)

Rituals mark beginnings and endings, allowing us to honor that which we are leaving behind and that which we may look forward to. Below is a ritual to acknowledge the change in the mother/daughter relationship when the daughter is grown. This ritual can be done together with the involvement of both mother and daughter or independently without the presence of the other. While the ritual does reference the use of a physical cord, please note that the ritual can be adapted so that rather than being a tangible object, the cord is envisioned.

Mother/Daughter Separation Ritual

This ritual allows you to connect with Demeter and acknowledge your independence in the mother/daughter relationship. Please note that the parts are written separately for the mother and the daughter as though it were a solitary ritual. However, this can be adapted to a combined ritual for mother and daughter to share in at the same time. All of our relationships with our mothers and daughters and different and have a myriad of dynamics. Recognizing this, I have tried to provide options for both mothers and daughters who still have a positive relationship as well as for mothers and daughters that have had a more complicated relationship and may not be in active communication. Feel free to adapt the statements in the ritual or to write your own. The exact words are not important so long as it is heartfelt and feels right to you.

Materials Needed:

A candle, preferably white, yellow, or blue.

2 strings or cords.

A small fireproof container or cauldron.

Pen and paper.

Something to purify the circle and yourself with. If you do not wish to actively energetically cleanse yourself and the area you will be working in, you can always put a bowl with sea salt on your altar as a purification tool. If you are not averse to scents, I would recommend adding essential oils such as rosemary, lemongrass, pine, lemon, peppermint, or lavender.

A representation of Demeter for your altar.

Offering for Demeter.

Optional: A picture or object to represent your mother or daughter.

Note: I recommend taking a warm bath with sea salts prior to undertaking this ritual as a way to relax and purify. This ritual can be emotional so be sure to take care of yourself afterwards and allow yourself plenty of time to process. You might consider journaling after the ritual.

1. Set the altar with all of the objects above.
2. Cast a circle using your preferred method.

3. Light the candle that you have chosen and place that on the altar.
4. Conduct active energetic cleansing (ie with incense or sound) if you have chosen to do so.
5. Take the cords or strings and tie one end of one around your waist and knot it. Take the other cord or string and tie it to the string around your waist with a knot so that it looks like a string tied to a balloon. Finally, tie a knot on the end of the second cord or string.
6. Sit in the middle of your circle and take some time to observe your breath.
7. Think about what your mother/daughter has taught you and what gifts they have given you that you wish to carry forward with you. These could be positive traits but if you had a more challenging relationship with your mother/ daughter, this might include wisdom that you have gained from a negative experience.
8. As you keep these lessons or gifts in your mind, state the following:

If you are the daughter, you might say something like, "I stand here no longer a child but an independent being in my own right. I hereby pledge my intent to separate my identity from that of my mother. I release you, and take with me the following gifts...." If you feel so moved, you might thank your mother for the gifts and/or wisdom that you are carrying forward.

If you are the mother, you might say something like, "I stand before you as a mother who recognizes my daughter's sovereignty as an independent being. I hereby release her to her own path and pledge my intent to birth my sovereignty anew beyond my role as a mother. I take with me the following gifts ..." If you feel so moved, you might thank your daughter for the gifts and/or wisdom of motherhood that you are carrying forward.

Untie the knot where the two cords meet and place the cord not tied around your waist inside gently. *Please note that this separation of cords does not have to equate to no longer having a relationship with your mother/daughter. It simply sends the message to the universe that you are acknowledging the separation and releasing your intent to move forward into a new phase of your life. Also, the act of separating the cords can be quite emotional, so please take time to grieve the separation and change in relationship with your mother/daughter as needed.*

With the pen and paper, write or draw what it is you wish to bring into this new phase of your life and/or how you intend to move forward. Standing before your altar, state aloud what you have written on your paper. Light the paper with the flame of the candle and let the paper burn to ash in a small fireproof container of cauldron. As you do so, remove the cord from your waist and state the following:

Daughter – "Demeter, I stand before you, a woman in my own right. I will ever be a daughter, but I no longer am a child. I ask for your blessings as I claim my sovereignty."

Mother – "Demeter, I stand before you, a mother who recognizes her daughter as a woman in her own right. I will ever be a mother, but I now embrace other opportunities as well. Like you, I contain multitudes and I ask for your blessings as I enter this new phase of my life."

Take a few moments to commune with Demeter, to reflect on the past and envision what you wish the future to be. Be sure to thank her for her guidance, gifts, and/or presence.

When you are ready, you may close the circle and leave the offerings in a sacred indoor or outdoor space for Demeter. If you wish, you may keep one of the cords as a reminder of the gifts you are carrying forward from your mother/daughter.

Journal Questions

- What aspects of the Demeter archetype do you most relate to? What aspects do you least relate to?
- Are there ways in which characteristics of the Demeter archetype may have been present in your relationship with your own mother? If so, how did this manifest and what impact do you think it may have had on you (both positive and negative)?
- How do you feel when you consider taking time for yourself and putting your own well-being first? If you have feelings of guilt, what do you think makes you feel this way?
- What would it look like if you were to provide yourself with the love and nourishment you need? What are some simple ways that you can begin to "mother" yourself?
- If you underwent the cutting cords ritual, how did it make you feel? What aspects were the hardest for you? What brought you the most satisfaction, peace, or joy?
- How can you use Demeter qualities to birth and nourish intangible aspects of your life, such as in your job or in creative expression?

Chapter 4

Demeter Chthonia: Grief and Loss

Few other goddesses deal with grief and loss to the extent that Demeter does. It is in her grieving aspect that she is most often known as Demeter Chthonia and is perceived as having a "... *gloomy, death-related aspect"*. (Downing, 1994, 12) While we tend to think of her daughter, Persephone, as being more closely related to the Underworld and its inhabitants, Demeter was also associated with death. In Athens, the dead were referred to as "Demetroi", or "Demeter's People", and it was she that received her worshippers when they died. (Spretnak, 1978) Even her epithet "Black Demeter" is believed to refer to the black mourning clothes she wore when grieving the loss of her daughter. (Carlson, 1997)

It is fair to say that while those who worshipped Demeter celebrated her maternal aspect, they also respected and honored her chthonic aspect. As the initiates in the Eleusinian Mysteries learned, life and death are but two halves comprising the whole. The acknowledgement of Demeter as a chthonic deity can be seen in the structure of her temple at Eleusis. Whereas most Greek temple sites were built above ground, the temple complex at Eleusis was built around a subterranean chamber which was within sight of the cave that was said to be the entry to the Underworld. (Downing, 1994) Many historians believe that the ritual that took place during the Thesmophoria also was imagined as having taken place in the Underworld. (Downing, 1994)

Demeter may not seem to be an obvious ally when it comes to time spent in the shadows mourning a loss. Yet, as I began to grieve the unexpected death of my young niece while writing this book, I found her to be an incredible source of solace, compassion, and strength. Despite being a goddess, Demeter is not above losing that which is most precious to her and feeling anguish as a result. Author Carl Kerenyi reveals that nature's principles can apply to deities as well as humans, for Demeter cannot avoid the universal experience of loss and suffering. (Downing, 1994)

Demeter's myth is in many ways a detailed description of the process of mourning. (Downing, 1994) In the "Hymn to Demeter", Helios tells Demeter that Persephone should put a stop to her great mourning and not grieve in vain because Hades will make a suitable husband for Persephone. (Shelmerdine, 1995) This, of course, does not assuage Demeter's pain in any way. Rather, the attempt to disregard her loss only intensifies what she is feeling. Homer states,

"But a more terrible and savage grief came into Demeter's heart..."
(Shelmerdine, 1995, 38)

Soon after, Demeter causes a famine on Earth. This physical famine in many ways mirrors the internal emotional famine that Demeter is experiencing. (Downing, 1994) Demeter appears to experience what Elisabeth Kubler-Ross calls the five stages of loss.

In their book entitled, "On Grief and Grieving", authors Dr. Elisabeth Kubler-Ross and David Kessler identify the five stages of loss that most people tend to go through when grieving. These stages include denial, anger, bargaining, depression, and acceptance. (Kubler-Ross, Kessler, 2014) It is important to note that the authors emphasize that these stages are not always linear, that they can be repeated, and that not everyone experiences each stage. Furthermore, while these stages refer to loss in the form of a death of a loved one, they can just as easily be applied to less tangible losses such as the loss of a job, a relationship, and/or a belief.

Denial is not necessarily a literal term. When someone we love is lost to us, feelings of denial do not mean that we don't know the person is gone; rather, it is more a sense of disbelief and a lack of acceptance of our new reality. Shortly after Persephone is taken, Demeter wanders the land in a state of shock and denial. Demeter is obviously very aware that Persephone has been abducted; she just refuses to accept that she will never see her again.

In addition, there is little evidence to suggest that Demeter has fully accepted that Persephone's abduction has also led to a loss of her own identity and sense of self. In some ways there are small, subtle signs that Demeter may have recognized this secondary loss for she disguises herself as an old woman – the antithesis of her identity as a fertile and nourishing young mother. Yet she still acts from a place of a mother responsible for her child(ren) and authorized to make decisions on their behalf. Despite having lost control over her own daughter's fate, she still believes it is within her right to control the fate of other children whose lives are in her care, such as Demophoon.

The second stage, anger, is clearly demonstrated by Demeter. This stage is particularly intriguing when you consider that, for almost 200 years, psychologists have theorized that depression is anger turned inwards. Whether or not this is accurate, there is evidence to indicate that it may be more socially acceptable – particularly for women – to show other signs of depression than it is to express what are very normal feelings of anger and rage in response to a significant loss. In Demeter's case, however, neither her expressions of anger or sadness are acceptable to most of the other deities she encounters.

Demeter is angry at what she feels to be the senseless loss of her daughter. She is offended by the advice given to her by Helios that she stop mourning and be happy about what has happened. She is filled with rage at the abduction to the point where she refuses to obey the authority of the almighty Zeus and instead unleashes her anger on the entire world by causing a famine on Earth. Demeter also lashes out at Metaneira when she is caught putting Demophoon in the fire.

It is not uncommon when we are grieving the loss of someone, we love to experience anger at ourselves. Even though we may know it's not rational, we may blame ourselves for not doing enough to prevent the loss. This can sometimes lead to self-punishment. It is therefore very possible that part of the reason Demeter clothes herself in black, diminishes her beauty and refuses to care for herself is that she feels she should have done more to prevent Persephone's loss and that she doesn't deserve self-compassion or beauty.

This bargaining stage can be characterized by a strong desire to undo what has been done and one may attempt to bargain with a higher power to reverse the loss. Guilt also accompanies bargaining as we ask ourselves, "what if I had done things differently?". (Kubler-Ross, Kessler, 2014). While we don't see Demeter outright asking these questions, she does in a sense bargain with Zeus for the return of her daughter via her willingness to end the famine when she is reunited with Persephone. The incident with Demophoon is also a subtle example of the stage of bargaining. By placing Demophoon into the fire to make him immortal she may be subconsciously attempting to protect him and Metaneria from the type of loss that she has experienced and could not prevent.

The next stage, depression, is a hallmark of Demeter's existence following the loss of her daughter. Demeter is the only one of the Olympic gods and goddesses to manifest symptoms that in this day and age would lead to a diagnosis of major depression. (Shinoda Bolen, 2002) As author Dunn Mascotti describes it,

"In the myth...Demeter...is seized by a terrible depression and feels as if she was buried in a hole, lacking purpose and sense of direction and she no longer knows how to employ her energies. Her

life becomes barren as in the myth she stops the seeds from growing until her daughter Persephone is restored to her." (1990, 167)

It is interesting to note that both Demeter and Persephone choose not to nourish themselves when they are first separated. In Homer's version of events, Persephone initially refuses food and drink offered to her by Hades when she is taken to the Underworld. The ancient Greek geographer, Pausanias, claimed that Demeter put on her black clothes and shut herself up in a cave in Arkadia as a result of her grief. (www.theoi.com/Olympios/Demeter) Demeter is also described as fasting and moving about as though *"propelled by pain and anger"*. (Burkert, 1985, 160)

There are various descriptions provided to us in the "Hymn to Demeter" that further illustrate the depth of grief and despair that Demeter is feeling. These include but are not limited to:

Not bathing
Not eating/loss of appetite
Disguising her beauty/not taking care of herself
Denial of reality
Feelings of hopelessness
Inability to envision a brighter future
Becoming withdrawn and focusing inward
Social isolation
Pulling away from family and friends
Crying a lot
Moving through the day without a sense of purpose
Tries to find things to distract her from her pain
Sometimes lashes out in anger when things don't go according to plan, when she's challenged, and/or sometimes without an apparent trigger
(Downing, 1994)

These symptoms not only pertain to depression caused by a physical loss but, as Alice Miller states, depression is also a defense against the pain that comes with losing one's self and one's identity. (Downing 1994) In Demeter's case, the depression-like symptoms she is experiencing are situational and are caused by deep grief.

Kubler-Ross points out that the next stage, acceptance, does not mean that the person grieving is okay with what has happened. (Kessler, 2014) Rather, acceptance refers to accepting that we have lost our beloved and our lives will never be the same. It is a process of reintegration and an attempt to readjust to our new reality. Allegorically, the Eleusinian Mysteries show us that death or loss is,

> "...a pre-requisite to the growth of the grain, that generation and fertility...are indissolubly bound up with death." (Downing, 1994, 65-66)

Acceptance does not erase the anguish that comes with loss. What it can do is to recognize the opportunity for creation and re-birth even in what may seem like the unending darkness. There are many examples of influential and life changing movements that have been founded as a result of someone's loss. Demeter, too, comes to this type of acceptance in the midst of her mourning as she gifts the people of Eleusis with the life changing Eleusinian Mysteries. She is also known for giving humankind gifts of agriculture and laws in her role as Demeter Thesmophoros.

Having lost my niece, two friends and a beloved animal companion in the course of two months this past year, there have been times when I have felt grief threaten to overwhelm me like a tidal wave; drowning me in my own despair. Having experienced the first four stages of grief – some simultaneously – I found myself turning to Demeter and asking for her wisdom and love. This resulted in a deep and powerful connection with Demeter in both her maternal and her chthonic aspects, and I was able to begin to heal through her lessons of surrender and rebirth. I have also learned to be a better ally and friend to others experiencing their own grief as a result of her lessons in holding space.

Surrender is a concept that I have had a love-hate relationship with for as long as I can remember. Perhaps because I had no choice but to rely on others for much of my childhood, when I finally attained my independence the concept of surrendering to anything or anyone was terrifying. It's not that I wished for control over others; rather, I was determined to control my own fate and was at times foolish enough to think that I could control everything in my life. Grief does not tolerate this kind of foolishness. Loss leaves you feeling powerless and grief leaves you little choice but to surrender.

It's not just the physical loss that we are forced to confront when we grieve, it is also the loss of the idea of how our lives are and were supposed to be. Often times in society, we are given unspoken rules about what is an acceptable period of time in which to grieve. After that time period has passed, we are often expected to pull ourselves up, dry our tears, and get on with our lives. Unfortunately, while these expectations are often shared with us by well-meaning loved ones, they are harmful and only exacerbate the emotional damage that has been done.

Demeter shows us that while there are some things we must let go of, grief is a necessary and natural part of this process that can't be rushed or ignored. We cannot experience acceptance or birth unless and until we have given grief it's time. (Kubler-Ross, Kessler, 2014) Demeter is wise to bristle at Helios' assertion that she should stop mourning and just be grateful for what has occurred. When Zeus sends multiple deities to try and cajole Demeter in getting back to her old activities and her old self quickly, she refuses. There is a tendency to isolate while we are mourning, for truly how can we ever adequately express the myriad of feelings that we are experiencing? How can we interact with others, pretending that nothing has changed?

Feelings of isolation are completely normal and healthy after a loss. Well-meaning friends and loved ones may encourage you to get out of the house and talk about your emotions. Sometimes people's desire for you to get back to "normal" and be social again may subconsciously have more to do with their fear, and/or feelings of awkwardness and discomfort. As difficult as it may be, we must let go of the instinct to make others feel more comfortable so that we can attend to our own needs.

We must allow ourselves the time and space to feel our loss as this is critical for our own well-being. It is important that we let go of arbitrary timelines for grief and healing. Grief is not a linear process. Even though Demeter's grief diminishes in the spring each year when she is reunited with Persephone, she still expresses her feelings of loss during the more barren winter when Persephone is no longer with her.

Similarly, we must let go of what we think grief should look like and how it should manifest. Everyone is different and there is no right or wrong way to grieve. Demeter surrenders to her despair and to her rage for perhaps she knows that if you fight or ignore your feelings of loss, you postpone the inevitable and you risk multiplying the pain at some point down the line. Grief is not a straight line. It's important not to get mired in it forever, but it's also important to honor our loss. The path out of grief is often comprised of baby steps and it's a path that often is shrouded in darkness for most of the journey. That's okay, for the darkness can also be our safe haven for a time; our cocoon. As Sharon Blackie states,

"...the finest plants push their way out of the deep, rich, fertile soil. Out of the darkness comes strength and focus. There is always

another rebirth. But it always begins in the dark. Be still, listen, let yourself disintegrate." (2019, 384)

The sadness and loss will likely never go away, and it may hit us years after the loss happens. Life may never be the same, but life does go on. It is important to grieve but we must also recognize when it is time to poke our heads out of the darkness. Although Sharon Blackie acknowledges the rich opportunities for growth and healing that exist in the dark, she also points out,

"One of the greatest dangers (of the dark) lies in the fact that it is all too easy to get stuck there. We may focus in too tightly on the intensity of our grief, sinking into it, drowning in it". (2019, 139)

The task, then, is to find a balance between resting and healing in the comfort of the shadows and knowing when it is time to begin to emerge into the light. This is where Demeter's lesson of rebirth can be beneficial.

Demeter teaches us how to heal from the depression and hopelessness that can accompany feelings of loss and/or violation. (Carlson, 1997) If nature shows us anything, it's that energy never truly dies but simply changes. Death clears the way for rebirth, and the fields that may seem barren now still have the potential to bring forth new life. In the initial stages of grief, this may seem like an impossible concept to embrace. We may feel guilty for even thinking about the possibility of rebirth. As Elisabeth Kubler-Ross asserts,

"The reality is that you will grieve forever. You will not 'get over' the loss of a loved one; you will learn to live with it. You will heal, and you will rebuild yourself around the loss you have suffered. You will be whole again, but you will never be the same." (2005, 230)

Nature is a constant cycle of life, death, and rebirth, and this is reflected in our lives as well. No matter how much we might try to stop time and subvert the cycle, it will continue. The only choice we have when the cycle swings back around and it is time for new growth to begin is whether or not we will choose to intentionally bring to life that which sustains us, contributes to our own well-being, and possibly even results in a "rebirth" in the form of a legacy for the person we have lost. If the lost loved one is someone that you had a complex or even difficult relationship with, it may be that you incorporate the lessons that you learned from that relationship to break a cycle within your own family or to provide yourself with the nurturing and love that this person was unable to provide.

Perhaps one of the most compelling lessons that Demeter provides us with is the healing power of compassion for ourselves and others as we emerge from our cocoon. Part of the healing process includes allowing us to feel love and compassion for ourselves just as much as we may have done in the past for others. This compassion gives us permission to move forward and to not feel guilty about moments of joy or happiness we experience despite our sadness. In some cases, the grieving person is hit with the realization that time is short and is not guaranteed, and takes that opportunity to do things that they have always wanted to do.

Suffering a loss could in some way inspire one to pursue a new vocation, a more loving relationship, or a healthier lifestyle. Sometimes when a loved one is lost, we find ourselves inspired to share their wisdom and gifts in helping others. This could include volunteering for a cause our loved one was passionate about, writing a book, and/or starting a foundation in our loved one's name. We might even let our anger fuel rebirth through advocacy efforts with legislators and/or within the community. Many powerful movements have been started as a result of a tragic loss.

The unexpected loss of my niece prompted me to finally

pursue certification as an End-of-Life Doula; something I had always been interested in but never thought to pursue. My family is also starting a foundation to honor my niece by providing funding for research for Addison's Disease and by offering scholarships to students in need who exhibit the characteristics of kindness and compassion that my niece possessed. These are just some of many ways in which new life may grow from a loved one's death.

Demeter shows us that those we have loved and lost never truly leave us. Demeter doesn't get to be in Persephone's physical presence all of the time, but Persephone is still there with her mother in some aspect and Demeter can be assured that reunion is guaranteed each year. According to Jennifer Reif (1999), Demeter "...*reveals the brilliant light of the infinite.*" However we choose to experience rebirth, our efforts further ensure that our loved ones live on. What is remembered, lives.

Just as it is important to allow ourselves the space necessary to grieve so that new life can manifest, my work with Demeter has also emphasized the need to be able to allow those around me to grieve in their own time and way as well. Often when we watch our loved ones going through the grieving process it can be painful because we want so badly to make them feel better and to ease their pain, but we don't know what to do. Demeter was fortunate to have someone who was willing to hold space for her and witness her pain. This someone was Hecate.

Shortly after Persephone's disappearance, Hecate comes to Demeter and tells her she heard Persephone's screams and agrees to help her find out what happened. Hecate accompanies Demeter on this journey. Unlike the other deities, Hecate doesn't judge or condemn Demeter for her grief and anger, and she doesn't try to convince her to hurry up the grieving process. She simply offers to help her find information and bears witness to her grief.

Simply accompanying others through their journey of grief

without offering advice or trying to counsel them can be a very difficult and uncomfortable thing to do. Yet, it is often the most effective way of supporting those we love when they experience a loss. Elisabeth Kubler-Ross tells the story of a woman, Wanda, who was grieving the loss of her twin brother. A month after her brother's death, her friend, Gail, told her that she needed to be strong. She invited Wanda to go shopping, telling her that she needed to get back out into the world. Wanda turned to Gail and said, *"'Gail, the real question is, do you have the strength to sit here with me in my sorrow?'"* (Kubler-Ross, Kessler, 2005, 103)

Many people in Demeter's myth attempted to "help" her out of her grief. Helios minimized her pain, and various gods and goddesses tried to cajole her out of her grief by offering kind words or gifts. None of these efforts worked and in some cases, they only further prolonged Demeter's pain and strengthened her resolve to withhold life while her daughter was being kept from her. Only Hecate possessed the wisdom to support Demeter in a truly healthy and loving way.

The best thing we can do for those we love who are grieving is to follow Hecate's example and hold space for others, walk beside them if they so desire, and bear witness. We can offer assistance or respond to requests for help if it's appropriate so long as we maintain solid boundaries and don't try to make the person feel better, pressure them to "hurry up" and get back to a normal life, and/or try to get them to look on the bright side. Both Demeter and Hecate act as guides for how we can best support others as well as ourselves through the mourning process.

Below is a meditation that came to me while I was communing with Demeter in some of my most painful moments of grief. It has provided me with a great deal of comfort and peace of mind and I hope that it may help you as well.

Sit in a quiet, comfortable space where you won't be disturbed. Focus on your breathing. Breathe in, breathe out. Now imagine a doorway in front of you. This could be any kind of door. When you are ready, step through the door.

You find yourself on a hill, overlooking the ocean. The sun is bright in the sky, and you make your way down from the hill over to an open space where there is a well. The vegetation is lush and includes a grove of ancient olive trees with their thick gnarled roots and bushy crowns of leaves and pomegranate trees with red, round crowned fruit. You walk over to a well which is surrounded by bay laurel trees and you inhale the pungent earthy scent of its leaves.

Soon, a woman walks towards you. She is tall, with golden blonde hair and she is wearing a simple, flowy long purple tunic that is draped over one shoulder. She appears to be glowing, and in her hands, she holds a lidded basket. She approaches you, introduces herself as Demeter, and asks you why you are here.

You tell her you have come to learn from her about letting go and for help in dealing with any grief or loss you may be experiencing. Suddenly, the sky turns dark and all of the vegetation surrounding you becomes barren so that the trees that were once so vibrant now have only greying, bare limbs where leaves once were. You feel a slight rain start to come down and when you look at the woman she has transformed. She now appears older and sad. She is wearing a dark hooded cloak and while you can't see as much of her face, you can make out graying, limp hair, dark circles under her eyes, and an expression of grief on her face.

Demeter tells you that as unfair as it may seem in the moment, loss is a part of life. Without death, there is no birth just as without birth, there is no death. She opens the basket and offers you the opportunity to surrender your grief. You feel the sadness of your loss rising up inside you and culminate in your heart.

Demeter lifts the lid from the basket. It is completely dark inside As you look down into the basket, you watch as the grief pours out of you in a tangible form and into the basket. You are patient, as is she, while you feel every last bit of grief that you have in you in this moment and watch as it makes its way into the basket. When you feel that you have surrendered all that you have to give of our sadness and feelings of loss in this moment, the lid closes.

You find yourself needing to sit down and process what you are now feeling. These feelings may include but are not limited to confusion, emptiness, or even relief. You watch as Demeter sets the basket down. She turns to the well, and scoops some of its water into a cup containing what appear to be herbs. She hands you the cup and you drink of it, almost greedily. You are thirstier than you realized and you can taste not just the freshness of the water itself but also hints of mint and barley.

Demeter reminds you that grief is not time limited, though healing does take place and our feelings may evolve over time. She encourages you to look into the well. You may see a symbol or a vision which can help you in your times of deepest grief. Or you may simply feel a loving embrace and a sense of momentary peace.

Demeter transforms back into the beautiful, glowing woman in the purple tunic. The sky starts to lighten as she digs a hole in the fertile Earth near the well. You watch as she pours the energy of your grief from the basket into this hole and then covers the hole up, as though she were planting a seed. She then waters the Earth using the water from her well. As you watch, the skies become even lighter and you begin to see subtle signs of life around you as though Spring is just starting to bloom.

Demeter smiles at you and embraces you lovingly and you feel her mothering energy and unconditional love surround you. After a time, she tells you that you may return to this place anytime that you feel the grief is too much and/or that you need her healing and love. Finally, she asks you to hold out your hands and she gives you a symbol of what you have lost to help you heal. This may be a special memory or symbol associated with a lost loved one. It could also be something that symbolizes all of the best of something intangible that you have lost – such as lessons learned from a job or relationship that you can take with you into your future and rebirth.

You know that your journey of grief is not over, but you also know that rebirth is possible in some way, shape or form and that you are loved and supported in this process. You take a moment to thank Demeter and when you are ready, walk back up the hill and through the door. Pay attention to your breathing. Wiggle your fingers and toes and when you are ready, open your eyes.

Journal Questions

- Think of a time when you experienced a loss of some sort. Did you take the time to grieve? If so, how did you grieve? In what way did acknowledging and feeling your grief help you to heal? If you did not take time to grieve, how did this impact your healing process?

- Are there losses in your life that you have not acknowledged or grieved? If so, what are they? Give yourself permission to grieve these losses. You may want to journal about how these losses impacted you and how your grieving process has played out.

- When you have experienced and mourned losses, how have you eventually moved on? Were there any new opportunities or efforts of "rebirth" that came out of this loss?

- It can be challenging to hold space for someone we care about who is grieving, particularly if we care deeply for this person and/or we have a strong desire to help. What are some ways you can hold space for someone without inadvertently interfering with their grieving process? What signs can you look for to catch yourself if your desire to help starts to go beyond holding space?

- What does holding space look like to you?

- Sharon Blackie talks about allowing ourselves to spend time in the darkness and "disintegrate". Have you ever allowed yourself to spend time in the darkness and/or fall apart, even for a brief time? If so, what did that feel like and how did you eventually move out of this space? If not, why do you think it is that you were unable to allow yourself to do this?

- Are there any rituals or practices that you have found to help you when you are in the midst of despair? Are there any rituals or practices that you might like to try?
- Think of a time when you had to heal from a significant emotional wound or loss. What personal skills, talents, or characteristics ultimately allowed you to heal and move forward?
- How can our society better support others in their grief?

Chapter 5

Demeter Chloe: Manifestation Magick

Demeter Chloe was one of the epithets of the great Mother Goddess. The title of Demeter Chloe refers to the goddess' association with fertility and her ability to manifest abundance. She is the goddess of intentional planting, nurturing, cultivating, and harvesting. (Carlson, 1997) Demeter embodies transformation; a critical ingredient in manifestation.

Demeter transforms and births both as the Goddess of Earth and in her aspect as a mother. As author Dunn Mascotti explains, when a woman is pregnant,

> *"...(she) multiplies herself into another being and becomes the channel for bringing another soul to life. For nine months, she creates matter, shapes a body, brings substance within herself like an alchemist transforming essence into living matter." (148)*

The cycles of nature mirror the cycles of our souls. Both the seed and the child spring forth, grow, and mature. At the end of their season of life, both plant and person die, creating the conditions for new life to begin in some form. (Reif, 1999) The cycle is eternal, for new life begins, grows, and dies and then is the source of its own rebirth. (Reif, 1999) The Eleusinian Mysteries incorporated a form of sympathetic magic in its rites by mixing seed corn with the decaying flesh of the pigs that were sacrificed, thereby connecting death and fertility. (Carlson, 1997) Similarly, the cycle of growth for wheat shows us that wheat is the source of its own regeneration. We, too, have the power to be our own source of rebirth and to manifest our desires.

Just as Demeter is responsible for helping humans to grow abundant crops, she can also help us to work with the energies of abundance and manifest what we wish to bring into our lives. This need not only occur when the external or internal seasons are at their peak, for Demeter's myth teaches us that life and growth can happen even in the darkest of times. In the Greek agricultural cycle, the pomegranate flowered in the early summer and ripened in the fall after the threshed grain had been stored in silos. (Reif, 1999) Ancient Greeks stored their grain necessary for human sustenance in underground silos during the barren season, indicative of a belief by the ancient Greeks that there was treasure to be found in the dark. (Corak, 2020). Demeter shows us that we can use our times of pain as times of gestation. This allows us to heal, to gain wisdom, and to focus our energies on rebirth and renewal. (Carlson, 1997)

The recipes and spells below will help you to connect to Demeter Chloe and manifest that which you wish to bring into your life. For any recipes containing herbs, be sure to seek medical advice before using if you suspect you may be pregnant or might have any allergies or adverse reactions. For oil recipes, be sure to use essential oils as opposed to fragrance oils which do not contain the same energies and can be irritating to skin. Because essential oils can also be a skin irritant for some, I recommend only using a small amount of anointing oil on skin or in baths to start to see how your skin reacts.

Demeter Chloe Oil Recipe

The oils in this recipe contain both fiery and earthy energies which resonate with Demeter and help to facilitate manifestation. Oils with a fiery tinge are often associated with the sun which nourishes growth and is necessary for life. The earthy energies of these oils are aligned with Demeter and symbolic of the womb from which all life springs – be it plant or human. Peppermint oil is associated with money and prosperity and driving away negative energies. Rosemary is an herb that was sacred to the ancient Greeks and is known for clarity, protection, purification, success, and banishing depression. Also known for easing depression, patchouli has long been associated with fertility magick and has a reputation as a powerful attractor of money and abundance.

Materials Needed:

Dark colored glass bottle with dropper top.
A carrier oil such as olive oil, grapeseed oil or sunflower oil
15-20 drops of Patchouli essential oil.
3-4 Drops of Peppermint essential oil (Peppermint oil can be quite strong. If you are not used to topical use of peppermint oil, I highly recommend starting on the low side of the range of drops suggested until you have a better sense of how your skin will react. You may also want to do a small patch test on the underside of your wrist. If peppermint oil is too strong for your skin, you may omit it from the recipe.)
10-12 Drops of Rosemary essential oil.

Fill the glass bottle ¾ of the way full with the carrier oil. Add the essential oils in the order shown under the materials needed list. Secure the lid firmly on the bottle and shake vigorously. This oil can be used to anoint candles, worn in aromatherapy jewelry, added to a diffuser, and/or added to baths.

Calendula Oil Recipe

The bright orange blossoms of the calendula flower lend themselves perfectly to manifestation magick. Orange is the color of creativity and the flowers themselves are reminiscent of the sun. Calendula's magickal uses include attraction, positive energy, success, prosperity, and nurturing. Calendula is relatively easy to grow and seems to thrive without a lot of maintenance. In addition, this flower is well known for being excellent for rejuvenating skin. Medicinally, calendula has a reputation for being anti-inflammatory, antiseptic, and a great detoxifier. This Calendula Oil can be used in the Manifestation Candle Spell below as well as an anointing oil hair conditioner, and skincare tool.

Note: If you are pregnant, please check with your health care provider before using this oil topically.

Materials Needed:

Jar with a lid
Dried calendula flowers or loose petals. (It is important that the flowers or petals be completely dry)
Carrier oil. (Grapeseed, Jojoba, Coconut, Almond and Olive Oils are all great choices)
Cheesecloth or some other straining equipment
Amber or another dark colored container

Steps:

1. Fill the jar halfway to three quarters of the way full with the dried calendula.
2. Fill the jar with your carrier oil until the jar is full or at least until the calendula is completely covered. You may want to take a wooden stick to poke the oil to rid the jar of air bubbles and ensure the flowers are covered.
3. Put the lid on the jar tightly and place the jar in a sunny windowsill. If you live in a climate that is extremely hot you may want to gently drape a towel or cloth napkin over the jar.
4. Every few days, roll the jar to mix the flowers and oil.
5. Let the mixture infuse for at least three to four weeks.
6. When you are done infusing, take a piece of cheesecloth or some other straining material and place it over the empty amber/dark colored container. Pour the infused mixture

over the cheesecloth into the empty container. When this is done, you may also want to place the remaining flowers in the cheesecloth and squeeze it into the jar to get the last remaining bits of oil that have soaked into the flowers. You can also leave the oil overnight and strain it again the next morning, but this is up to you.

7. Keep the oil in a cool, dry, dark place. You may want to consider transferring some of the oil into an amber dropper or pump bottle for ease of use.

Simple Manifestation Candle Spell

Candle spells are some of the most effective and efficient ways to work magick. With this simple spell, you will want to have a clear vision of what it is you wish to manifest. If this is a short-term goal or if you are unable to attend to the candle for very long, I would recommend using a small chime candle as they tend to burn down within a couple of hours. If what you wish to manifest has a longer time period, you may wish to use a jar candle, pillar candle, or 7-day candle. Whichever type of candle you use, please be sure to never leave your candle unattended.

The color of candle you use will depend on your goal. If you are attempting to manifest prosperity, I would suggest using a green candle. Pink candles work well for focusing on manifesting self-love. If you wish to manifest a job or a promotion, red or green are good choices. If you are living in chaotic times and wish to manifest greater stability and peace, blue or white might be what you choose. Orange and yellow are great colors for manifesting creativity, energy, confidence, and for manifestation work in general. The most important factor is what you associate colors with. For example, if the color green doesn't make you think of abundance but brown does, then be sure to go with your gut and use brown.

Materials Needed:

1 candle and candle holder.
Sun oil (see recipes above)
Herbs and/or flowers (optional)
Something to carve symbols into the candle

Hold the candle in your hands as you visualize what it is you wish to manifest. When you have a clear picture in your mind, imagine transferring the vision and the energy of the vision into the candle. Next, using a needle or some other inscribing tool, carve symbols or words into your candle which represent what it is you wish to manifest. Alternatively, you could write words or draw symbols or pictures representing your goal on a piece of paper and place this under the candle holder.

Rub the sun oil on the candle while you continue to envision your intention for the spell. Many practitioners rub the oil from the top to the middle of the candle and again from the bottom to the middle of the candle when focusing on manifestation. I have found dressing the candle from bottom to top three or more times to be just as effective when working manifestation magick as I envision the energy moving upwards and into the universe. Use whichever technique resonates most strongly with you. If you wish to dress the candle in herbs and/or flowers as well, simply roll the candle in the herbs or flowers you have chosen. There are Demeter aligned herbs included in Chapter 8; however, don't feel you have to limit yourself to these suggestions. Be sure to pick herbs that align with your intent. For example, patchouli and/or mint tend to work well for manifestation of money.

Finally hold the fully dressed candle in your hands and ask Demeter for her assistance in this work. You can use the invocation below or you can write one on your own.

Demeter Chloe, Great Mother
She who brings life into being
She who helps all things to grow

I ask you to aid me in my goal
So that I may manifest _____ into my life
As surely as you manifest the bounty of Earth
May I nourish that which serves me and the gifts that are given to me
As surely as you nurture all living things under your domain
May my harvest be successful as I walk in your path
Hail Demeter!

Place the candle in the candle holder. For added effect, you might consider placing the candle holder itself in a shallow bowl filled with the Sun Water you have made. Burn the candle while focusing on your intent. When the candle has fully burned down, you may wish to practice ceromancy by pouring the hot wax from the candle into the bowl of Sun Water and watching for images to form.

Sun Water

Sun water is very easy to make and can enhance any magickal workings for manifestation. Sun water can act as a booster for your confidence in your ability to manifest and to help you focus on what it is you desire. Sun water can be used in many ways including added to a bath, anointing one's third eye, and consumed by adding a drop or two to a glass of water. If you are feeling creative, you can use sun water with watercolor paints and paint a picture of what you wish to manifest.

Materials Needed:

Mason jar or another container with lid
Spring water
Something to write or paint with (optional)

Pour the spring water into the mason jar or other container. As you pour the water in, try to focus on what you wish to charge this water with. For example, you might concentrate on qualities of confidence, clarity, and/or energy to help you carry out your manifestation magick. If you have a clear desire of what you wish to manifest and you will be using this water solely for that purpose, I recommend writing down what you wish to manifest or creating a picture or symbols to represent your goal and placing the paper around the jar so that the picture or writing is facing the water inside. You can also paint or write directly on the jar.

Put the lid on the container and place the water directly outside in the sun or on a windowsill that gets a good deal of light. The best time to do this is when the sun is at its peak but if that is not possible any time during the day will do. For best results, leave the water to charge for no less than an hour and no more than eight hours. When the water has charged, place it in a cool, dark space in your house. You can place it in the refrigerator as well. You can also place the sun water on your altar to Demeter to further enhance its power.

Journal Questions

- What would you like to manifest in your life within the next year? Within the next five years? How do you think manifesting these things will contribute to your success, well-being, and/or overall happiness?
- What skills, talents, knowledge, and/or attributes can you use to help nurture that what it is you wish to manifest?
- What are you willing to give up in order to create space for manifestation to occur?
- What practices make you feel confident and abundant? How can you incorporate these things into your life more regularly, especially when you are focusing on manifesting something new?

Chapter 6

Demeter as Law-Giver, Advocate, and Warrior

As we have seen, Demeter is a very complex, multi-faceted goddess. She is best known for her loving, nurturing aspects yet there are many myths and components of myths wherein Demeter is not so calm and peaceful. There is another side to the Mother archetype beyond being gentle and loving which is typically referred to in our society as the "Mother Bear". The Mother Bear is known to call upon great reservoirs of strength and fierce courage if she feels that her children are threatened in any way. It's interesting that our culture tends to accept women that are strong and outraged on behalf of their children given that in general our society sometimes invalidates or condemns women who appear to be angry or even assertive on their own behalf or the behalf of someone other than their children.

Demeter is not generally an angry or punishing goddess; at least, not without reason. Typically her anger and retribution is reserved for times when something or someone important to her is violated or dishonored in some way. (Carlson, 1997) As Stephanie Carlson reveals,

"She becomes negative only to those who uphold the patriarchal order, never to her daughter and only when dishonored or after Kore or she herself is raped." (1997, 62)

In lesser-known myths, we do see her more vengeful side unrelated to the circumstances Carlson notes. Still, when Demeter enters her aspect of "Erinyes" or "Melaina", there is usually some component wherein a male figure dishonors or disrespects her or her daughter in some way. In the myth of Erysichthon, she punishes the son of Triopas for cutting down an ancient fir in her sacred grove despite his men advising him not to. According to the myth, the tree cried aloud when it was cut and Demeter cursed Erysichthon with a cruel, insatiable hunger that plagued him to the point that he eventually ate himself. (www.theoi.com/ Olympios/Demeter.html)

Lynkos, the King of Skythia, was transformed by Demeter into a lynx when he tried to kill Triptolemos, son of Metaneira and King Keleos. Karnabor, a king of Northern Greece, also dishonored Triptolemos by killing the flying serpents that drew his chariot. Demeter sent a pair of beasts to destroy Karnabor, ultimately placing him among the stars with the title of "Ophiokhos", or "Serpent Holder". Askalabos, a man of Argo, was changed into a lizard after he mocked Demeter for her "ravenous drinking of meal" when she rested while looking for Persephone. (www.theoi.com/Olympios/DemeterWrath)

Another male Argo citizen, Kolontas, was said to have been burnt in his house by Demeter because he would not help Demeter when she asked for his hospitality as she searched for Persephone. In some versions of the story of Demeter and Persephone, it was an Underworld demon by the name of Ascalaphus who informed Hades that Persephone had eaten the pomegranate seeds. As punishment, Demeter turned Ascalaphus into a lizard. While they are few, there are some stories in which Demeter's punishment falls on other females.

Minthe was an Underworld nymph who was once Hades' lover. Hades left Minthe for Persephone which caused the nymph to be jealous. Minthe attempted to win Hades back and maligned Persephone, a transgression for which Demeter transformed her into the mint plant. There is also a myth that asserts that a group of Sirens was transformed into bird-like monsters for refusing to help Demeter find her daughter. Yet, some interpret this myth as the transformation having been welcomed by the Sirens. (www.theoi.com/Olympios/

DemeterWrath) The Erinyes associated with Demeter were also thought to appear as monsters with wings of a bird but there does not appear to be any evidence to connect the Erinyes with the transformation of the Sirens.

The term Erinyes is purported to come from the Greek words, "to stir or excite" or "to be in a rage". Thus, Erinyes describes both an emotional state and a mythical being. Akin to the Furies, the Erinyes were said to be female creatures who lived in the Underworld and sought to right wrongs and avenge crimes. It is unclear specifically how they were connected to Demeter though some theories suggest that they were the servants of either Demeter or her daughter, Persephone.

Some ancient Greeks believed that they were the spirits of crime victims – particularly those who were murdered – who would haunt their assailants and drive them mad. (Carlson, 1997) The Erinyes were known to be particularly outraged at the murder of a mother. (Carlson, 1997)

The Erinyes are mentioned in Iliad as being, "...*invoked in oaths and their terrible power is harnessed to curses and harming magic...*". (Burkert, 1985) Rape was another crime that infuriated the Erinyes as, from their perspective, this type of forceful power imposed on the feminine was seen as out of alignment with nature and a dishonor to the Great Mother. (Carlson, 1997)

These female monsters are depicted as being gruesome and terrifying just as our own anger can be terrifying, particularly if not provided with a healthy outlet. The madness of the Erinyes is depicted as something to fear, avoid, and perhaps even something to subdue. How odd, when we consider the insanity and chaos that runs rampant in our world! Sometimes, anger is the best and most understandable response to the injustices that exist all around us.

So why is it that anger is not seen as an allowable reaction for women in a patriarchal society? There have been numerous articles in well-known publications including "Psychology

Today" that address this phenomenon. According to Sharon Blackie,

"Inside us, those old stories whisper, there might well reside a sleeping madwoman: a woman who cannot and will not tolerate the brutalities of the world around her. They suggest to us that one day...this madwoman within us might break out. More importantly, they tell us that at some point in our lives it might be okay to let ourselves break...to express our rage and lick our wounds..." (2019, 125)

Even Demeter, a powerful goddess, is not able to hold herself together and wear the mask of pleasant acceptance that is expected of her when faced with the injustice of her daughter's abduction. Demeter shows us that it is okay to fall apart at times, and that anger and grief are perfectly natural responses to actions that dishonor and/or harm us, those we care for or humanity in general. At some point, we must overcome and heal our wounds and realize that they do not define us. We must, at some point, find a way to use our anger for the greater good. However, in order to do this with authenticity and sincerity we must be willing to first confront and listen to the madwoman within. Meeting this shadow aspect of ourselves and giving ourselves permission to express our anger – albeit in a nonviolent way – can facilitate profound transformation and initiate the warrior within us who is determined to make things right.

Demeter's desire to hold those in power accountable and challenge the patriarchal ideals that can cause harm can be seen in her unwillingness to allow crops to grow so long as Persephone remains Hades' captive. Despite Zeus being known as the most powerful of Greek gods, Demeter is able to resist his requests and subvert his power. (Carlson, 1997) Demeter's qualities of stubbornness, patience and perseverance are assets which we can cultivate within ourselves as we move from her vengeful aspect to her role as law-giver. As is illustrated in Demeter's defiance and ultimately her triumph over Zeus, these qualities can influence powerful men and powerful institutions. (Shinoda Bolen, 1990)

Demeter Thesmophoros is Demeter the law-giver. This aligns well with her role as the Mother Goddess and Goddess of Agriculture, for as Christine Downing says,

> *"As a goddess who introduced humankind to agriculture, Demeter is associated with the establishment of polis-centered society. Cities are the gift of Demeter... many scholars have seen (her title meaning) ...'one who gives pleasing ordinances to cities'... as implying a recognition of how a stable, social world derives from the settled life of cultivators." (1994, 12)*

It is reasonable to assume that when the ancient Greeks became farmers, their effectiveness relied in part on their ability to interact and cooperate with others in their community to ensure a successful harvest. In addition to teaching mankind about agriculture, Demeter may also have shared productive ways in which to govern their work. Under the epithet of Thesmophoros, Demeter became the goddess of law and order and the deity who taught mankind the importance of laws. Given her role as a goddess of the Earth and working in balance with nature to foster a healthy farming cycle, it is easy to imagine that not only was Demeter concerned with man's law, she was likely as concerned if not more concerned with laws or actions that align with nature's principles. Demeter understood that sometimes the laws created by man – or in her case, by other gods – were not always just and could do more harm than good.

Whereas Demeter Erinyes may provide us with the fuel to enact change, it is Demeter Thesmophoros that helps us to understand the very systems that we must sometimes disrupt if we are to transform our society into one that is more just and which provides equitable access to opportunities and resources which allow everyone to experience well-being and fulfill their highest potential. There are many ways to embody Demeter Thesmophoros. It is important that you ask yourself what it is you are passionate about and/or what it is you wish to change. Advocating for transformation can come in many forms, which include but are not limited to:

Learning about how legislature works and using this knowledge to testify at legislative sessions for proposed laws
Writing or calling your legislator
Creating art that informs and inspires. This could be any type of art including writing, painting, sculpture, dance, music, or theater
Incorporating books about social justice topics in your child(ren)'s library
Working with a local non-profit on a cause that interests you
Changing your purchasing habits and/or daily routine to better reflect and align with the change(s) you wish to see occur

This is by no means an exhaustive list. Truly one can find a way to embody Demeter Thesmophoros in just about any role or aspect of their lives. Speaking your truth can be difficult, particularly given that women are often taught by society to keep the peace and not do anything that might rock the boat. Embodying Demeter Thesmophoros can be intimidating, especially if you are used to being the peacemaker and/or not sharing your opinions. Below is a recipe for an amulet that can help you to find the courage to speak your truth and persist even when met with resistance or disapproval.

Demeter Thesmophoros Amulet
The items that go in this amulet all act in some way to increase

your courage, stand your ground, feel centered in your purpose, provide strength, and speak your truth. Yellow citrine is reminiscent of the sun and is a good stone for success. Citrine has a reputation for being able to transmute negative energy into something that is positive. Onyx is a grounding stone which provides protection and feelings of strength and stability even in the midst of emotional turmoil.

In addition to looking like liquefied sunshine, amber promotes a positive attitude, confidence, and soothes the nerves. Red Carnelian is linked to personal power, courage, fertility and the fiery energies of transformation. Turquoise is an excellent crystal for opening your throat chakra and allowing full expression. Likewise, lapis lazuli is also a throat chakra stone which strengthens communication, self-expression and mental clarity.

You may have heard the saying, "Rosemary for remembrance". Rosemary is indeed a good herb for mental clarity and focus. Chamomile can help to ease one's nerves. An herb sacred to Greeks, oregano promotes joy, creative expression, serenity and protection. Oregano is also used to cure ailments associated with the throat chakra such as coughs. The personal symbol that you choose to add to this amulet should be one that symbolizes courage, communication, and/or transformation. A small figurine of a snake or actual shed snakeskin is one such symbol as it is associated with Demeter and represents transformation. Other possibilities might include a dragon, a bear, a scepter, or a picture of someone you admire for their strength and candor,

Materials Needed:

Small bag or pouch. Blue is a great color choice, but other colors will do as well.
1 piece each of citrine, onyx, amber or red carnelian, and turquoise or lapis lazuli

1 pinch of rosemary

1 pinch of chamomile

1 pinch of oregano

A representation or symbol that you associate with courage, strength, communication, and/or transformation. (optional)

1. Place the objects in the bag or pouch as you envision yourself speaking your truth confidently.
2. Hold the amulet to your throat, followed by your heart and the area just below your stomach.
3. Ask Demeter Thesmophoros to bless the amulet to provide you with the strength and confidence necessary to share your opinions and enact change.
4. Charge the amulet on your altar or in a sunny place for one full day if possible.

Carry the amulet with you whenever you feel the need to draw the strength of Demeter Thesmophoros.

Journal Questions

- What is your perspective and laws and rules? Do you feel that they should be followed strictly to the letter, that they are more guidelines and intent is more important than actual language, or do you fall somewhere in between? Why do you think this is?
- What are you passionate about? What injustices make you the most upset?
- What are some ways you can use your knowledge, experience, and/or talents to get involved in a cause related to your passion(s)?
- What personal rules do you live by? How have these rules helped you? Are there any ways in which they have hurt or inhibited you?

Chapter 7

Bridging Both Worlds: A Ritual to Connect With and Honor Demeter

The ritual mirrors the cycles of death and rebirth and embodies Demeter's role as both the grieving mother and the mother who manifests new life. The purpose of this ritual in addition to connecting with both light and dark aspects of Demeter is to draw upon her lessons and wisdom to release something you have lost or which no longer serves you and to manifest what you wish to fill the void with. It is believed that Demeter's priestesses wore white chitons. You may want to wear something loose and flowy in light of this, but be sure to take precautions when working with flames so that loose sleeves or other items of dress do not catch fire.

Materials Needed:

Purification item (This can be sacred water, incense, or a bundle of loose herbs tied together to form a smoke bundle that can be safely lit. Rosemary, bay laurel, and thyme are all good choices.)
1-3 seeds
A cornucopia (you can usually find inexpensive ones at arts and crafts or dollar stores, especially in the fall. However, you can use a basket in place of a cornucopia.)
A sheaf or two of wheat (this can also usually be found inexpensively at arts and crafts stores.)
Plantable seed paper, or, if you prefer, 1-3 actual seeds. I suggest using seeds for plants that are easy to grow and maintain.
Potting soil

Planter

Collage or drawing to represent what it is you wish to manifest

Cauldron or small fireproof container

Paper and pen

Demeter Anointing Oil (recipe found in Chapter 8)

Candle

Representation of Demeter. This can be the sheaf of wheat, a statue of her, a small pig or snake figurine, a picture, or whatever resonates for you and helps you to develop a connection with Demeter.

Fresh fruit and/or vegetables or fresh flowers to place in the cornucopia or basket.

Prior to conducting the ritual, create a visual representation of what it is you wish to manifest in your life at this time. I would suggest limiting your manifestation goals to no more than three for this ritual. You can paint or draw directly on the planter or you can make a drawing or collage on a separate piece of paper. If you choose to do the latter, tape or glue your picture/collage so that the visual images are facing the inside of the planter.

Begin by setting up the altar. On the left-hand side of the altar, place the cauldron and candle. In the center of the altar, place your representation of Demeter and the sheaf(s) of wheat. On the right-hand side of the altar, place the cornucopia or basket filled with your offerings of fresh fruit, vegetables, and/ or flowers.

Begin by purifying yourself and your sacred space using sacred water, incense, or your smoke bundle. If you are using water, wash your hands lightly and anoint yourself at your third eye, your throat, your heart, and your womb area or just slightly below your stomach. If you are using incense or a smoke bundle, be sure to either place the incense or bundle in a fireproof container and stand over the smoke or wave the smoke around you. Anoint your third eye, throat, heart, and womb or stomach with the Demeter anointing oil.

Cast a sacred circle by first imagining your feet connecting to the core of the Earth and pull up Earth energy through this connection. Imagine a golden light coming up through your body. When you feel completely connected, imagine a cord rising up from the top of your head up through the sky and imagine a silver-colored light flowing down through your body through this cord. Now, imagine the gold and silver lights merging together at your heart. Concentrate on sending this merged energy from your heart into your hands until you can strongly visualize or feel the energy between your hands.

Moving clockwise, place your hands up with your palms outward and imagine the energy flowing from your hands as you envision a circle being formed by the Earth element that is sacred to Demeter. This could be a circle of trees, corn, or some other tall vegetation or flower. Walk the circle nine times clockwise in honor of the nine days that Demeter spent looking for her daughter. Once the circle has been cast, you may want to take some time to chant, settle into your breathing, or simply commune with Demeter in your own way.

When you are ready, light the candle on the altar. Taking pen and scraps of paper, write down 1-3 things that you have lost recently and/or are letting go. These should be things that are important to you in some way. This could include things like the physical loss of a loved one, the loss of a job, or the disappointment of having something you were hoping for not manifest (or at least not in the way you wanted). Hold the scraps while you concentrate on what you have lost or are letting go and what that means for you. Take time to grieve and honor your loss.

Once you have taken the time you need to grieve, using the candle's flame light each scrap of paper and then put them in the cauldron or fireproof to burn. You may want to state something like the following:

_____ *I honor you as I acknowledge our separation. I thank you for the lessons, gifts, happiness and/or love that you have given me. I release you with love.*

Feel free to share any other thoughts or heartfelt words that you feel are appropriate. Once the scraps have fully burned, snuff the candle on your altar.

Next, turn your attention to what you wish to manifest. If you are using plantable seed paper, write 1-3 things you wish to manifest in your life on the paper. If you are using seeds, lightly draw a symbol on each seed to represent what it is you wish to manifest. State the following,

"Great Demeter, Mother of Earth, She who gives life and turns the barren fields fertile
Hear me as I share my intent to bring my desires to fruition
I intend to birth _____ into my life (name what you have written on the seeds or paper that you wish to manifest
I plant these seeds into fertile soil
Just as you birthed your daughter, Persephone, and brought life into being
I, too, will birth these desires
Just as you nourish your children of bone and blood and your flora
I, too, will nourish these desires
Just as you have let go, I let go of any doubts about my success
I ask for your guidance and blessing in this endeavor
Help me to draw upon my gifts, talents, and courage to nourish what I wish to bring into being
Help me to find the strength and endurance to bring what I have planted to life
Guide me so that I may see opportunities that might otherwise be hidden

Bless me with your abundance and your love"

Fill the planter with potting soil. Plant the seeds or plantable seed paper in the soil according to instructions. As you plant the seeds or paper, state aloud what it is you wish to manifest.

Note: Sometimes people have concerns about attaching manifestation desires because they worry that if the plant doesn't flourish or die, what they wish to manifest will not come to fruition. If this is a concern that you have, you may place the seeds in the soil to symbolize your intention and when the ritual is over you can take the seeds out of the soil and leave them on the altar or place them in a small bag that you can carry with you as a talisman.

Now, state what you intend to nurture your "plant" with. For example, if you are manifesting a new job you might state, "I commit to fertilizing this desire by applying for 5 new jobs a week."

If your goal is more intangible, such as wanting to increase your confidence, you might say something like, "I commit to nourishing this desire by writing down one thing I accomplished each day and one thing I am good at."

Once you have completed these statements, take a moment to visualize your desire(s) manifesting in your life. If you are intending to grow a live plant with your seeds or paper, you may wish to water it according to instructions with spring water that you have charged with your intent. If you are using plantable seed paper and intend to grow wildflowers in an outside spot, you can remove the paper from the soil and plant it outside.

Close your circle by walking counter-clockwise nine times and visualizing the trees, corn, or vegetation descending into the ground.

When you are done, be sure that there are no longer any lit flames and leave your offering of fruit, vegetables, and/or flowers in a spot you deem sacred. I typically leave mine outside under a tree and then compost them when they have decayed.

Chapter Eight

Walking the Path: Additional Methods for Connecting with Demeter

Correspondences

Other Names or Titles for Demeter: Horaphonis (Bringer of the Seasons), Polyphorbias (All Nourishing, Bountiful), Aglaocarpus (Giver of Goodly Fruit), Callistephanus (Beautiful Crowned), Eustephanus (Lovely Crowned), Eucomus (Lovely Haired), Xanthe (Blonde, Golden Haired), Callisphyrus (Beautiful, Trim Ankled), Dia Thea (Bright Goddess), Semne (Holy, August, Revered), Hagne (Pure, Chaste, Holy), Anassa (Queen Lady, Potnia Theaon (Queen Amongst Goddesses), Cydra Thea (Glorious, Noble Goddess), Agane (Venerable), Epaine (Awesome), Demeter Panagia (All Holy Demeter), Demeter Chioaia (Verdant Goddess), Demeter Chloe ("Blooming", "Fertility"), Demeter Antaia (Demeter Besought by Prayers)

Similar deities: Ceres (Rome), Auset/Isis (Egypt)

Family Tree:
Mother – Rhea
Father – Cronus
Grandmother – Gaia
Grandfather – Uranus
Brothers – Zeus, Poseidon, Hades
Sisters – Hera, Hestia

Children: Persephone (Zeus); Despoina, Aerion and the Erinyes (Poseidon); Ploutos and Philomelos/Bootes (Iasion); Euboleos and Khrysothemis (Karmanor)

Lessons: Abundance, Motherhood, Letting Go, Authenticity, Independence, Growth, Sovereignty, Death and Rebirth, Transformation, Personal Power, Dealing with grief, loss, and depression, Manifestation, Fertility, Boundaries

Archetypes and Roles: Mother Goddess, Initiator, Earth Goddess, Law Giver, Avenger

Sacred Sites: In Greece – Eleusis, Kerameikos Cemetery in Athens, Temple of Demeter in Naxos, Hermione (in Argolis), Attica, Arcadia, Sanctuary of Demeter Erinyes in Ocium. In other countries – Temple of Demeter in Selinus, Sicily; Rock of Ceres, Sicily; Also, wheat fields, gardens, wells

Symbols: Cornucopia, Torch, Lidded Basket (Cista Mystica), Bread, Wheat, Scepter, Plough, Chalice (for holding the sacred Kykeon drink)

Trees: Oak, Poplar, Willow, Fir, Pomegranate, Myrtle

Herbs: Pennyroyal, Mint, Laurel, Patchouli, Rosemary, Lemon Thyme

Flowers: Rose, Poppies, Jasmine, Orange Blossom, Calendula, Crocus, Daffodil, Hyacinth, Larkspur, Delphinium

Crops: Wheat, corn, barley, various fruits and vegetables

Other food offerings: Honey, Sweet Cakes, Bread, Corn, Wine, fresh fruits and vegetables, Galaxia (a milk and barley porridge)

Stones/Crystals: Citrine, Amber, Garnet, Rose Quartz, Red or Orange Carnelian, yellow Topaz, Pyrite, Onyx, Jasper

Colors: Gold, Yellow, Orange, Red, Pink, Green, Beige (the color of wheat), Black (in her grieving aspect)

Animals: Pig, Snake, Gecko, Screech Owl, Turtle Dove, Red Mullet (fish regarded as sacred to Demeter in the Cult of Eleusinian Mysteries)

Mythological Creatures: Dragons (Dragons were said to pull Demeter's chariot in Ovid's version of her myth) (Downing, 1994)

Holy Times/Festivals:
Thesmophoria (Fall)
Eleusinian Mysteries. The Lesser Mysteries were conducted in what we know as February or March whereas the Greater Mysteries were conducted in September
Chloia (early Spring)
Kalligenia (Spring)
Thargelia (mid to late Spring)
Skirophoria (Midsummer)
Stenia (Early Fall)
Thalysia (Fall)
Proerosia (Fall)
Rites of Nestia (Fall)
Arkichronia (Mid to Late Fall)
Haloa (Winter, most likely in December)

Types of Magick: Abundance/Fertility, Growth, Releasing/ Letting Go, Shadow Work, Self-Love, Self Confidence, Clarity, Grief, Persistence, Resilience, Manifestation, Mother/Daughter relationships, Creativity, Death and Rebirth, Vengeance, Justice/Advocacy

Elements:
During the Light Half of the year: Earth, Fire

During the Dark Half of the year: Water

Types of Music:
Demeter's aspect in the Light Half of the year: Drums, flutes, lively music
Demeter's aspect in the Dark Half of the year: Dirges, violins, somber music

Tarot Correspondences:
Demeter's aspect in Light Half of the year: The Empress, Queen of Pentacles

Demeter's aspect in the Dark Half of the year: The Hermit, Death

Chant – *"Demeter, Great Mother"*
Demeter, Great Mother
Demeter, Great Mother
Demeter, Great Mother
Fill me with your love
Let the seed take root and grow
Nurturing and powerful
Let the seed take root and grow
And flourish with your love"

Below are recipes for a sugar scrub and anointing oil. Be sure to use essential oils as opposed to fragrance oils which do not contain the same energies and can be irritating to skin. Because essential oils can also be a skin irritant for some, I recommend only using a small amount of anointing oil on skin or in baths to start to see how your skin reacts.

Demeter Sugar Scrub

Using a sugar scrub to exfoliate is not only healthy for your skin, but it can also be a form of sympathetic magick in that you are shedding your skin and letting go so transformation can begin. Both peppermint and rosemary have invigorating properties. Peppermint is said to drive off negative vibes. Rosemary, a solar herb, is purifying. Rose is good for the skin and has a very loving, gentle energy. Rose is also known to symbolize new beginnings.

Materials Needed:

Non-metallic Mixing Bowl
Glass container with a lid
1 cup of sugar
½ cup of carrier oil. Possible options include Extra Virgin Olive Oil, Almond Oil, Grapeseed Oil, or liquid Coconut Oil
8-10 drops of Peppermint essential oil
10-15 drops of Rosemary essential oil
6-8 drops of Rose absolute essential oil

Mix the sugar and carrier oil in a bowl. Add the essential oils and flowers and mix again. Pour the scrub into the container and keep out of sunlight. Use during baths or showers.

Demeter Anointing Oil

This anointing oil aligns with the energies of Demeter in her nurturing, mothering aspect. In addition to helping you to build a connection with Demeter, it also possesses gentle energies of compassion, self-love, and support. Roses have magickal properties traditionally associated with love, purification, emotional healing, and forgiveness. Rose essential oil has the highest frequency and vibration of any essential oil, which is fitting as we attempt to raise our own vibration and step into our power.

Neroli oil gives off a very refreshing and sensual scent and can aid us in working through emotional challenges. The oil helps to ease tension and create an atmosphere of joy and optimism.

Additional properties include relieving pain, melting tension, and reducing anxiety and depression. Rose and Neroli essential oils are good for sensitive skin. Both Rose and Neroli oils may seem like gentle oils but are very powerful, albeit in a more subtle way.

As we work to let go of that which no longer serves us or that which may have been taken away from us, we may find ourselves being critical of our past choices. Rose's ability to aid in self-forgiveness combined with Neroli's energies of serenity and love can be very effective and calming as we do any kind of work related to loss, pain, and/or grief. (Corak, 2020)

On a metaphysical level, this energy can be very soothing as we work to love ourselves and heal our wounds. Patchouli, an earthy oil, has properties of fertility, love, healing, and releasing and is also known to be an antidepressant.

Please note that pure essential oils of Rose such as Rose Otto can be very expensive. I would recommend looking for rose absolute oil as that tends to be less expensive and just as effective. Alternatively, you could also make rose oil using the same base recipe for Calendula Sun Oil presented earlier in this book by simply substituting roses for the calendula.

Materials Needed:

> Dark colored glass bottle with dropper top
> A carrier oil such as olive oil, grapeseed oil or almond oil
> 10-12 drops Neroli essential oil
> 15-20 drops Rose Absolute essential oil
> 2-3 drops Patchouli essential oil

Fill the glass bottle ¾ of the way full with the carrier oil. Add the essential oils. Secure the lid firmly on the bottle and shake vigorously. This oil can be used to anoint candles, worn on skin, worn in aromatherapy jewelry, added to a diffuser, and/or added to baths.

Chapter Nine

Demeter's Bounty

Given Demeter's domain over the crops that sustain and nourish us, cooking a feast in her honor offers an effective way to deepen our relationship with the Mother Goddess. The Greek myths are filled with stories wherein food plays a central role, including but not limited to the nectar and ambrosia which is typically only consumed by the gods. It is not uncommon for deities within the Greek pantheon to be associated with various items of food and drink such as Dionysus with wine and the lesser god Priapus with vegetation and livestock. Demeter is most well known for her association with crops and grains such as breads, wheat, and corn products. The recipes below incorporate foods with a Greek flavor that include ingredients that are either symbols of Demeter or can facilitate our connection with Demeter and her myth in some manner. *Recipes contributed by Steven Corak*

Multi Grain Bread

8 ½ Cups Bread flour
2 ½ Cups water
1 Cup multigrain mix
3 Tablespoons Honey
2 Tablespoons Dry active yeast
2 Tablespoons milk
2 Tablespoons Olive oil
1 ½ Tablespoon salt
Semolina Flour as needed

For the multi grain mix you can use whatever combination of grains, seeds and or nuts you desire. For this recipe I recommend using a mix of sunflower kernels, pumpkin seeds, brown flax seeds, golden flax, black and white chia seeds, and hemp kernels.

Combine yeast with ½ cup warm water mix in ½ cup of the bread flour to create a sponge. Allow yeast to bloom for about 20 minutes. Combine the rest of the flour with salt and create a well in the middle of the flour. Add milk, oil, honey, sponge, grain mix, and 2 cups of warm water. Mix the dough until it forms solid mass, adding additional water if the dough is too dry. Transfer to a work surface dusted with semolina flour and knead for 5 to 10 minutes. The dough should be smooth and not stick to your hands. Place dough in a greased bowl and cover with plastic wrap to allow it to double in size. This will take approximately 1 ½ to 2 hours. Punch down dough and divide into 3 pieces, working them into desired shape and knead for a few minutes. Ferment the loaves in a warm environment covered loosely with a dish towel for one hour. Do not over-ferment. Score the tops of the loaves and bake at 450 degrees for 25 to 30 minutes.

Harvest Bounty

2 cups farro
1 Cup cream
¾ bunch kale
1 bunch parsley chopped
8 oz caper berries
6 oz goat cheese
¾ Cup green olives sliced
½ Cup Kalamata olives sliced
½ cup olive oil
½ cup pine nuts
¼ cup buttermilk
4 oz Calabria peppers
6 cloves garlic, chopped
2 tablespoons oregano, chopped

2 Tablespoons salt
1 Tablespoon pepper

Combine cream, goat cheese and buttermilk. Heat on medium high heat, stirring regularly. Simmer for 15 minute or until you have a rich creamy sauce. Add in oregano. Season with salt and pepper to taste.

Next, combine olives, peppers, ¼ cup of olive oil, caper berries, garlic, parsley, pine nuts, and black pepper and roast at 350 degrees for 20 to 30 minutes. De-stem the kale and chop it into small pieces. Then, place the chopped kale in a sealable plastic bag with ¼ cup olive oil and 1 tablespoon salt. Massage kale by gently pounding it with your fists, mixing in oil and salt until the kale is a vibrant green color and soft.

Bring 1 gallon of water with 1 tablespoon of salt to a boil and add the farro. Cook until soft, about 30 minutes. Drain water. Combine the farro, hot olive mixture, and kale and mix until fully incorporated. Serve with your favorite grilled meat if desired. Drizzle goat cheese sauce over top.

Serves 4.

Golden Apple Spiced Cake

For the cake:

2 Cups flour plus 2 Tablespoons
1 ½ Cups sugar
1 Cup Canola oil
4 eggs
2 Golden apples, finely diced
¾ Cup walnuts, chopped
½ Cup milk
½ Cup currants
¼ Cup brown sugar
3 Teaspoons cinnamon

2 Teaspoons Vanilla

1 Teaspoon baking powder

½ Teaspoon baking soda

½ Teaspoon salt

¼ Teaspoon ground cloves

¼ Teaspoon Allspice

¼ Teaspoon Nutmeg

For the topping:

1 Golden apple, thinly sliced

2 Tablespoons sugar

2 Tablespoons melted butter

In a mixing bowl cream eggs with sugar until fully mixed. Add in the oil, milk, and vanilla and continue mixing. In a separate bowl, combine 2 cups of flour with 2 teaspoons of cinnamon, baking powder, baking soda, salt, and all other spices and mix completely. Add flour mixture to the wet ingredients and continue mixing.

Then, combine walnuts, currants, 2 tablespoons of flour and mix together. Fold the mixture into the batter. Combine diced apples with 1 teaspoon cinnamon and brown sugar and fold this mixture into the batter also. Spread the batter amongst two greased loaf pans and top with sliced apples. Brush the tops of the loaves with the melted butter and sprinkle sugar over top. Bake at 350 degrees for approximately 1 hour. Test to see if it is ready by inserting a toothpick into the cake. If the toothpick comes up clean, the cake is ready.

Conclusion

Despite Demeter's myth originating thousands of years ago, her myth still contains lessons that are relevant in today's world. Author Jennifer Reif asserts that even though we are no longer a society primarily comprised of those who work the land, our modern world still needs what is at the very heart of Demetrian Paganism; the knowledge that nature facilitates life and teaches us about our soul's growth. (1990) Demeter is still a fitting goddess for our times. The difficulties faced by Demeter include themes of victimization, grief, depression, anger, the fight for self-sovereignty and struggles for power and control. (Shinoda Bolen, 1990)

Sadly, these themes are still present in the lives of many women in contemporary society. Demeter can empathize with our struggles and can offer wisdom to help us with these challenges. She can help us to realize our inner strength and access the confidence and courage to stand in our power. She can also teach us when and how to let go. Through Demeter's myths, we learn how to give ourselves permission to feel and express our anger at the injustices we and others have faced so that we may then funnel these feelings into advocating for positive change. Demeter's arms can embrace us when we are mired in sadness and despair and provide a safe space for grieving, for she knows what it is like to lose that which is most precious.

While Demeter empathizes with our feelings of anguish, she also gives us hope for the future. As Jennifer Reif states,

"Through Demeter's myth we learn that there is always reunion. That which we have loved remains a part of our soul." (5)

Demeter's lessons can be daunting and they require a willingness to come face to face with our shadow self and inner demons.

Yet as a result of our journey with Her, we emerge stronger, more confident, and more powerful than ever. We recognize the power of the mother, the great creatrix within. There have been times in my work with Demeter when the grief and sorrow I was experiencing felt as though it would pull me under. Despite the sometimes-intimidating nature of my journeys with Demeter, I have always felt her light in the midst of the dark and have emerged from the journey stronger and with a greater sense of peace. As a result, I find myself better able to transform my pain into purpose and to use it in ways that make me stronger, happier, and able to serve the greater good. This is my hope for you dear reader as well.

As with any relationship, the more you work with Demeter, the stronger your relationship with her will be. There are many ways in which you can incorporate your work with Demeter in your spiritual practice. These include but are not limited to:

- Answering the journal questions in the earlier chapters of this book
- Looking back and reviewing past journal entries and reflecting on the progress and/or changes that have occurred
- Making an altar dedicated to Demeter
- Anointing a candle for Demeter with the Demeter anointing oil in Chapter 8 and lighting the candle for a bit each day as you sit at your altar
- Meditating on Demeter's lessons
- Visiting Demeter and her sacred sites in meditation
- Reading various versions of Demeter's story
- Chanting for 5-10 minutes each day using the chant in Chapter 8 or your own chants
- Set aside a space outdoors or on a windowsill to grow and care for a plant or two. You might want to consider

growing one of the Demeter aligned flowers or herbs
listed in Chapter 8

- Place 1-2 drops of Sun Water in your drinking water each
  day and take a moment to commune with Demeter and
  thank her for her guidance and gifts as you drink the
  water

- Cooking is also an act of creation! If you like to cook or
  bake, intentionally focus on how each step of the culinary
  process aligns with the way in which Demeter offers her
  gifts to the world. You might even consider dedicating a
  meal in her honor

If you are interested in a deeper, ongoing connection you might
also consider working with her various aspects by mentoring
children or young adults, finding an avenue for creative
expression, and/or getting involved with a cause that you are
passionate about. If you have a garden, you could also dedicate a
section to Demeter and grow herbs, trees, and/or flowers sacred
to Her.

Demeter can be a strong ally and mentor as you move through
the cycles of your life. If you start to feel lost, let Demeter's torch
help guide your way. If you find yourself crumbling under
the weight of despair, seek the Great Mother and let her arms
embrace you. In those moments where you may not feel that you
are strong enough, good enough, or just "enough", let Demeter
show you the bounty of gifts, strength, and beauty that exist
within you.

The Voice of Demeter

My purpose in writing this book has been to honor Demeter and
share what I have learned from working with Her in hopes that
it may help others as well. Demeter is not only a mother in the
traditional sense; she is a mother to us all in the spiritual sense.
In her roles as nurturer, avenger, and law giver, she seeks to help

all of humanity grow, live in right relationship with the land and with others, and realize and fulfill our highest potential. This is particularly true for those who she views as her daughters. (To be clear, my understanding from Demeter is that this term is not bound by gender.)

I felt compelled as I neared the end of writing this book to reach out to Demeter and find out if there were any messages she wanted to share. After communing with Her during a pathworking, I was left with the following message which I am blessed to share with you. It served as one last reminder for me as well, for I was initially surprised at the fervor contained within the message. The message holds energies of motherly love to be sure, but it also compels us to tap into her aspects as Demeter Erinyes and Demeter Thesmophoros. I should not have been surprised because as Demeter indicates in the message below and as I have stated throughout this book, Demeter is a complex, multi-faceted goddess and that is perhaps what makes her so fascinating and relevant to our modern lives.

Dearest daughters,
The time has come for us all to embrace our power as mothers and as manifestations of the divine feminine, for we alone have the power to birth new life into this world. There are some who would try to make us meek but we are formidable. There are some who would try to make us reliant on them, but we know we can rely on ourselves.
Nourish yourself. Rest in the darkness under the light of the moon. Own your power under the light of the sun. Let your voice be heard and let your truth be spoken, for you have the ability to bring the world to its knees if you so choose, just as I did when I defined the almighty Zeus. For where would we be without our mothers? Who protects their children more fiercely than a mother bear?
There are some who would underestimate us. There are some who wish for us to be no more than submissive ornaments that sacrifice for them, enable them, obey them. But we contain multitudes within us. It is

time that we let go of that which harms and birth new life, new visions, new ways of being into this world. Rise up and allow your voice to be heard. Make barren the unjust systems that do more harm than good so that a new and better future may occur.

Just as a mother teaches her child(ren) right from wrong, so, too, must we teach those who would subdue us. We teach with persistence, with patience, with fortitude, with firmness, and, yes, always with love. Find your allies; those who would stand with you just as Hecate stood by me. Those who see the need for change and who understand that inequities and injustices harm us all, even those who would seem to benefit. Come together to plant the seeds for a new and bountiful harvest that feeds ALL, not just a select few.

Mother yourselves just as you have mothered others. As difficult as it may be, sacrifice what stands in the way of your own well-being and soul's growth just as you have sacrificed for the benefit of others. Look. Look at yourself and be in awe of who and what you are. Feel your power. Recognize the mother spirit within you and the ability to manifest and bring forth new life, be it a child, a business, art or a movement. Appreciate your ability to nurture and to provide the conditions that allow yourself and others to prosper and blossom.

Just as the sun nurtures the fragrant rose, the vibrant poppies, and the life sustaining crops, know that I am here. Know that I am with you. I am the law giver, leading you to justice. I am the Erinyes, giving you permission to feel your anger and transform it into fuel and motivation. I am the companion in the dark to hold the torch and share your pain as you walk through the dark valleys of grief and loss. I am the mother, here to guide you through our own cycles of birth, death, and rebirth in your life.

I am here to hold you close when you feel lost. I am here to help you find your way. I am here to nurture you so that you may bloom. I am here to provide you with unconditional love and acceptance when you need it most.

Feel my light strengthen you.

Let my arms embrace you.

Let my love empower you.
Let my story and my presence lead you to find the divine that exists
within you.
Daughter
Mother
Goddess

Journal Questions

- Having completed this book with what aspect of Demeter do you now feel you resonate with most? Why do you think this is?
- What have you learned about yourself throughout this journey with Demeter?
- What aspects of Demeter's message resonated with you? What aspects, if any, provided you with new perspectives?
- How can you embody Demeter in your daily life to help you achieve your goals?
- How would your life be different if you were acting from a place of pure authenticity and honoring all parts of yourself? What would a typical day look like? How would you feel?
- Where are you at in the journey of loving yourself? How can you "mother" yourself and provide yourself with more unconditional love and acceptance? Think about small, simple things that you can do every day as these things may add up to potentially make a significant impact in the long run.
- Who, in your life, cares about you but may be inadvertently expressing their concern for you in a way that is not supportive of your independence and authenticity? What are some ways you can address this issue? What boundaries do you need to create?
- Take a look at the suggestions for connecting with Demeter on a daily basis. Which suggestions resonate

with you? What additional ideas do you have? Pick one idea to incorporate into your daily practice for the next lunar cycle. You may want to keep a journal to record your experiences with this practice.

- Look back at your journal entries for questions starting with Chapter 1. What have you learned throughout this journey? How have your perceptions and/or beliefs changed?

About the Author

A practicing Pagan for over 20 years, Robin Corak is the author of the Moon Books Pagan Portals title "Persephone: Practicing the Art of Personal Power" for which she was nominated for the 2020 Witchies award for "New Author of the Year". Robin has presented locally and at national conferences including Paganicon, Pantheacon, the A Year With Our Gods conference series, and the SOA Ninefold Festival. A longtime member of the Sisterhood of Avalon where she currently serves as the Board Secretary, Robin has also had her writing published in multiple anthologies and currently writes a blog for Agora Patheos entitled "Phoenix Rising". She has several years of experience with modalities such as Reiki, coaching, and tarot reading and is currently pursuing certification as an End-of-Life Doula. Passionate about helping others achieve their full potential, Robin is also the CEO of a large, non-profit social services organization in Washington state.

You can find Robin's website at www.phoenixawenrising.com

Bibliography

Athanassakis, Apostolos N.; Wolkow, Benjamin M. *The Orphic Hymns.* (Baltimore, MD: John Hopkins University Press, 2013)

Blackie, Sharon. *If Women Rose Rooted.* (Denmark: September Publishing, 2019)

Breton Connelly, Joan. *Portrait of a Priestess: Women and Ritual in Ancient Greece.* (Princeton, NJ: Princeton University Press, 2007)

Burkert, Walter. *Greek Religion.* (Cambridge, MA: Harvard University Press, 1985)

Caldwell, Richard S. *Hesiod Theogony.* (Newbury Port, MA: Focus Publishing, 1987)

Carlson, Kathie. *Life's Daughter, Death's Bride.* (Boston, MA: Shambhala Publishing, 1997)

Corak, Robin. *Persephone: Practicing the Art of Personal Power.* (Winchester, UK: Moon Books, 2020)

"Demeter" *Encyclopedia Britannica.* www.britannica.com/topic/Demeter

Downing, Christine. *The Long Journey Home.* (Boston, MA: Random House Publishing, 1994)

Dunn Mascotti, Manuela. *Goddesses.* (New York, NY: Barnes and Noble Press, 1990)

Gaba, Sherry. "The Mother Wound". October 25, 2019. www.psychologytoday.com/us/blog/addiction-and-recovery/201910/the-mother-wound

Geldard, Richard. *The Traveler's Key to Ancient Greece.* (Wheaton, IL: Theosophical Publishing House, 2000)

Kubler-Ross M.D., Elisabeth; Kessler, David. *On Grief and Grieving: Finding the Meaning of Grief Through the Five Stages of Loss.* (New York, NY: Scribner, 2005)

Lorre Goodrich, Norma. *Priestesses.* (New York, NY: Harper

Perennial, 1989)

Mark, Joshua J. "Isis". February 19, 2016. www.worldhistory. org/isis

Mierzwicki, Tony. *Hellenismos*. (Woodbury, MN: Llewellyn Publishing, 2018)

Opsopaus, John. *The Oracles of Apollo*. (Woodbury, MN: Llewellyn Publishing, 2017)

Preka-Alexandri, Kalliope. *Eleusis* (Athens: Ministry of Culture Archaeological Receipts Fund, 1997)

Reif, Jennifer. *Mysteries of Demeter: Rebirth of the Pagan Way* (York Beach, ME: Samuel Weiser Inc., 1999)

Serena Merto, Maria. *Death in the Greek World: From Homer to the Classical Age* (Norman, OK: University of Oklahoma Press, 2012)

Shelmerdine, Susan C. *The Homeric Hymns* (Newburyport, ME: Focus Publishing, 1995)

Shinoda Bolen M.D., Jean. *Goddesses in Every Woman: A New Psychology of Women*. (New York, NY: Harper Perennial, 1984)

Shinoda Bolen M.D., Jean. *Goddesses in Older Women: Archetypes in Women Over Fifty*. (New York, NY: Harper Perennial, 2002)

Spretnak, Charlene. *Lost Goddesses of Early Greece: A Collection of Pre-Hellenic Myths* (Boston, MA: Beacon Press, 1992)

"The Ancient Greek World: Daily Life Women's Life". *Penn Museum*. www.penn.museum/sites/greek-world/women. html

Wasson, R. Gordon; Hofmann, Albert; Ruck, Carl A.P. *The Road to Eleusis: Unveiling the Secret of the Mysteries*. (Berkeley, CA. North Atlantic Books: 2008)

You may also like

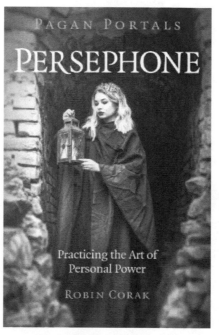

Persephone
Practicing the Art of Personal Power

Embark upon a powerful journey with Persephone, Queen of the Underworld and Goddess of Spring, as she helps you to discover your personal power and take control of your life.

978-1-78904-333-4 (Paperback)
978-1-78904-334-1 (ebook)

MOON
BOOKS

PAGANISM & SHAMANISM

What is Paganism? A religion, a spirituality, an alternative belief system, nature worship? You can find support for all these definitions (and many more) in dictionaries, encyclopaedias, and text books of religion, but subscribe to any one and the truth will evade you. Above all Paganism is a creative pursuit, an encounter with reality, an exploration of meaning and an expression of the soul. Druids, Heathens, Wiccans and others, all contribute their insights and literary riches to the Pagan tradition. Moon Books invites you to begin or to deepen your own encounter, right here, right now.

If you have enjoyed this book, why not tell other readers by posting a review on your preferred book site.

Recent bestsellers from Moon Books are:

Journey to the Dark Goddess
How to Return to Your Soul
Jane Meredith
Discover the powerful secrets of the Dark Goddess and
transform your depression, grief and pain into healing
and integration.
Paperback: 978-1-84694-677-6 ebook: 978-1-78099-223-5

Shamanic Reiki
Expanded Ways of Working with Universal Life Force Energy
Llyn Roberts, Robert Levy
Shamanism and Reiki are each powerful ways of healing; together,
their power multiplies. *Shamanic Reiki* introduces techniques to
help healers and Reiki practitioners tap ancient healing wisdom.
Paperback: 978-1-84694-037-8 ebook: 978-1-84694-650-9

Pagan Portals – The Awen Alone
Walking the Path of the Solitary Druid
Joanna van der Hoeven
An introductory guide for the solitary Druid, *The Awen Alone* will
accompany you as you explore, and seek out your own place
within the natural world.
Paperback: 978-1-78279-547-6 ebook: 978-1-78279-546-9

A Kitchen Witch's World of Magical Herbs & Plants
Rachel Patterson
A journey into the magical world of herbs and plants, filled with
magical uses, folklore, history and practical magic. By popular
writer, blogger and kitchen witch, Tansy Firedragon.
Paperback: 978-1-78279-621-3 ebook: 978-1-78279-620-6

Medicine for the Soul
The Complete Book of Shamanic Healing
Ross Heaven
All you will ever need to know about shamanic healing and how to
become your own shaman...
Paperback: 978-1-78099-419-2 ebook: 978-1-78099-420-8

Shaman Pathways – The Druid Shaman
Exploring the Celtic Otherworld
Danu Forest
A practical guide to Celtic shamanism with exercises and
techniques as well as traditional lore for exploring the Celtic
Otherworld.
Paperback: 978-1-78099-615-8 ebook: 978-1-78099-616-5

Traditional Witchcraft for the Woods and Forests
A Witch's Guide to the Woodland with Guided Meditations and
Pathworking
Mélusine Draco
A Witch's guide to walking alone in the woods, with guided
meditations and pathworking.
Paperback: 978-1-84694-803-9 ebook: 978-1-84694-804-6

Wild Earth, Wild Soul
A Manual for an Ecstatic Culture
Bill Pfeiffer
Imagine a nature-based culture so alive and so connected,
spreading like wildfire. This book is the first flame...
Paperback: 978-1-78099-187-0 ebook: 978-1-78099-188-7